D1645114

PORTRAIT OF CAITHNESS
AND SUTHERLAND

Portrait of
CAITHNESS
and
SUTHERLAND

by

James Miller

ROBERT HALE · LONDON

© *James Miller 1985*
First published in Great Britain 1985

ISBN 0 7090 2377 4

Robert Hale Limited
Clerkenwell House
Clerkenwell Green
London EC1R 0HT

British Library Cataloguing in Publication Data

Miller, James, *1948–*
 Portrait of Caithness and Sutherland.
 1. Caithness—Description and travel—
 Guide-books   2. Sutherland—Description and
 travel—Guide-books
 I. Title
 914.11'604858   DA880.C1

 ISBN 0-7090-2377-4

Photoset in North Wales by
Derek Doyle & Associates, Mold, Clwyd.
Printed in Great Britain by
St Edmundsbury Press, Bury St Edmunds, Suffolk.
Bound by Hunter & Foulis Ltd.

Contents

Illustrations

Photographs by the
author

Acknowledgements

I am grateful to Professor Derick S. Thomson of Glasgow University for permission to include his translation of Rob Donn's verse on p. 157; to J.M. Dent & Sons Ltd for permission to quote from Samuel Laing's translation of *Heimskringla*, revised by Peter Foote and published in the Everyman Library, on p. 38; to John Humphries, Caithness Books, for permission to use the extract from 'Peats for Power' by Castlegreen (Donald Grant) from *Tatties and Hereen*; to Jim Begg for permission to quote from his poem 'The Partan' on p. 100; to Jim Johnston for permission to quote from his article on Smoo Cave on p. 156; to Bette McArdle, Editor of the *John O'Groat Journal*, for permission to quote from that newspaper; to Penguin Books for permission to quote from Hermann Pálsson and Paul Edwards's translation of *Orkneyinga Saga* on p. 71 published in the Penguin Classics edition.

Introduction

The two counties of Caithness and Sutherland make up the most northerly part of the mainland of Scotland. Unlike the Hebrides, Orkney or Shetland, they remain relatively unknown to outsiders. They share some of the features of these, their northern neighbours, but Caithness and Sutherland have their own unique attributes. A great skelp of territory, of moor, mountain, field and forest, they are truly a land where cultures mingle: border country, where the northern frontiers of Celtic Scotland met the southward push of Norse expansion a thousand years ago.

To describe the two counties adequately in one book is no easy matter. I have imagined taking the reader on a journey, north along the east coast, west to Cape Wrath and then back south again down the west coast. There are also several forays inland to see some of the things to be found there, but much of the interior is empty of people and without roads. Most travellers will probably follow the coastal route or something close to it, and to some extent this book is a guide. I have assumed that the traveller will journey by car. If venturing north by bicycle, an excellent way to see the country, it would be wiser to travel clockwise from west to east – that way, the wind is more likely to be in your favour. There is much to discover and this will be a journey at a genteel pace and with many digressions – which is how any journey should be for the enquiring traveller.

I should also point out that it is 'a' portrait. I have focused on what is of interest to me, and I hope that I may be forgiven by those who question my eclecticism. I have devoted considerable space to historical events and contemporary topics that might not be obvious to the newcomer. There is much more to tell, and there are excellent local guides available that go into more detail on specific localities.

I owe a debt of gratitude to many people who patiently answered my many enquiries, particularly Alan Finch, Robert Howden, Alex Jappy, Jim Johnston, Joseph Johnston & Sons Ltd, J.K. MacGillivray, George McRobbie, Paul Reid, Bill Ritchie, L.J. Rowe, Elliot Rudie, the Reverend James A. Simpson, Tom Simpson, D.A. Thomson, Dr Eric Voice and William Wilson. I also want to thank Jack and Marie Hay of Evelix for their hospitality, and James Henderson, the Editor of *The Northern Times*, for invaluable corrections and suggestions.

There are others who gave me unstinting help without giving their names, and to these people I also owe thanks. Finally, I should make it clear that I have used all the information in this book in my own way, and I am responsible for any errors.

James Miller
June 1985

1

The Province of Kat

The best way to approach the north is by the A836. This road climbs gradually from the Cromarty Firth, skirts the head of Strath Rory, passes the lonely Aultnamain Inn and reaches its highest point, at about 700 feet, on the shoulder of Struie Hill. Here the road bends and dips to the west and, suddenly, far below lies the ten-mile sweep of the Dornoch Firth and, beyond, the hills of Sutherland. On a clear day, from the viewpoint by the road, the traveller can identify the distant massif of Ben More Assynt, and the summits of Ben Klibreck and Beinn a'Bhragaidh with its distinctive monument to the first Duke of Sutherland. It is a place to stop, to savour the landscape, to watch the Firth change its colours and moods as the clouds pass and the tides contest, leaving straggling foam lines across the surface of the water.

Up here, the presence of man seems slight. Apart from distant houses, no more than specks of colour, and the pylons striding over the ridge, the land looks much as it might have done to those who knew the country beyond as the province of Kat.

In 1915 Caithness and Sutherland were paired politically as a single parliamentary constituency, but this belies the differences between them. In fact, since the reorganization of local government in 1975, neither has technically been a county at all but Districts of the great Highland Region with its capital at Inverness. The inhabitants have, however, shown a healthy disregard for the niceties of government and, in all but name, as two counties Caithness and Sutherland remain.

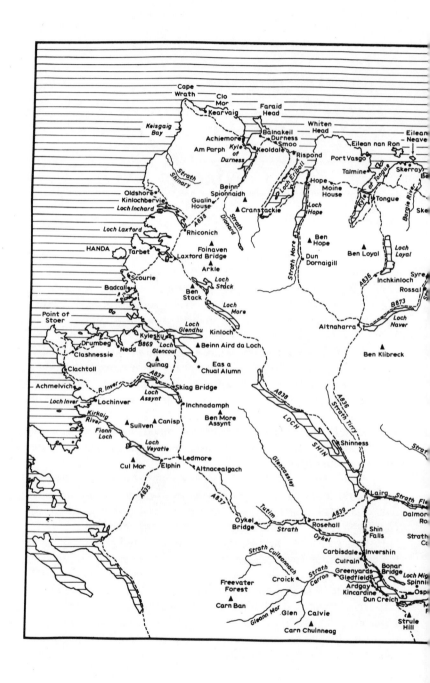

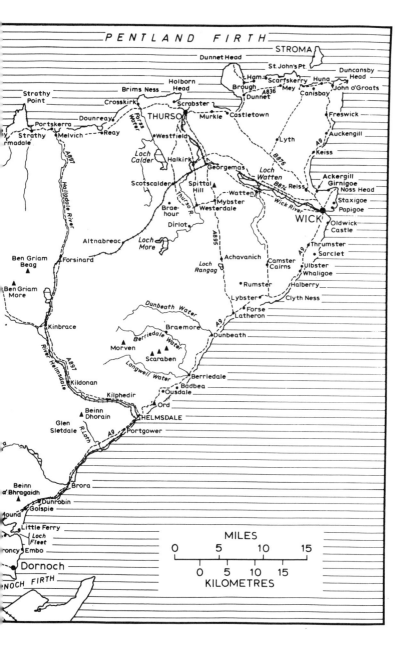

This map is reproduced with permission of the Ordnance Survey

One feature that will strike the traveller immediately is the relative scarcity of people. There are no cities. The four largest towns – Thurso, Wick, Brora and Golspie – have between them a population of about 25,000; the rest of the folk live in scattered townships, villages and farms. The population of Sutherland in the 1981 census numbered 14,241; Caithness was rather more densely peopled, with 27,380. These figures should be remembered in relation to the area of the two counties: Sutherland is over two thousand square miles, and Caithness almost seven hundred. Together, they make up one third of the Highland Region.

Despite the latitude, the climate is mild. The average winter temperature at Cape Wrath is 4.5°C, and palm trees grow in the garden of Scourie House twenty miles to the south. The North Atlantic Drift, creeping across from the Caribbean, warms the coast and ensures this mildness. Away from the sea, the temperature range is more extreme: Lairg has an average January temperature of only 1.1°C, compared to 12.7°C in August. The coldest temperatures recorded in Sutherland, down to –19°C, have been measured at Lairg; but summer frequently brings hot days over the 30°C mark. The average temperatures for Wick vary from 3.3°C in January to over 12°C in July, and the average for the whole year in 1983 was 7.75°C.

The coolness is compensated in summer by the extreme day-length. Clear weather at the end of June means almost no darkness, midnight golf for those who wish to indulge in the sport.

Rainfall is high on the coast facing the Atlantic but becomes progressively less as one travels east. The mountains in Assynt can be drenched in over 118 inches per year, but the annual rainfall at, for example, Dornoch is less than thirty inches. April and May are statistically the driest months but the visitor should be ready for changeable weather at any time.

The wind is the climatic factor of greatest importance to most people, especially on the west and north coasts. The air is hardly ever still. Cape Wrath has about thirty-eight days of gales in a year; most of them happen in winter, but even in summer strong breezes can still comb the land and churn the sea and lochs into whitecaps. The mean annual wind speed at Dounreay is nineteen miles per hour; for comparison, the figure for Kew Gardens is a gentle nine. The average wind speed at Wick in 1983 was 11.4 knots; the highest gust, recorded in January, was sixty-nine.

'The blighting wind that almost perpetually devastates Caithness', as Alexander Sutherland described it in 1825, is one reason for the absence of trees in many parts of the two counties, and the often weird shapes of those that do manage to grow. In the sheltered eastern valleys, however, there are some splendid woods, and the Forestry Commission has established plantations in many areas.

In winter, blizzards do not disrupt life for more than a day or two, though when the whirling white invader does strike, it is often brutal. In a severe blizzard in 1955, service helicopters were used for the first time in civilian rescue work. I remember one incident in Operation Snowdrop, as it was called, when a helicopter flew over our village to take to hospital a woman who had fallen on the ice and broken her leg. The school was closed for what seemed weeks to a seven-year-old, and we had a grand time sledging. For, despite the latitude, near the coast snow does not lie for long before melting in the salt-laden air.

Winter is also a time of great beauty, particularly when a frost holds the land in icy stillness and the light has a hard-edged crystalline quality during the short day. Also, if you are lucky, you might catch sight of the evanescent curtains of the Aurora Borealis, 'the merry dancers' as we call them, colouring the sky with pink and orange.

Wind and soil, too much of one and too little of the other, make many parts of the north at first glance a bleak, forbidding place. Those used to the soft downs of England may find these bare, rolling hills alien. The poor soils are the results of glaciation. About eighteen thousand years ago, the land was fast under a tremendous thickness of ice, which in its slow, ponderous march tore away the existing skin of soil and scoured the earth to its very bones. The glaciers went through phases of advance and retreat but finally melted away around ten thousand years ago. Since then, soil formation has been hampered by the climate. About one third of Sutherland and maybe half of Caithness are covered in peat, vegetation unable to decompose in the cool, wet environment. Much of the land is arable, however, and has been producing crops for centuries; and more of the 'hill', as the moors are generally called, awaits reclamation. In the west of

Sutherland there are large areas where the soil is too thin either to be reclaimed or to permit peat-cutting. But there are exceptions here too, particularly where a band of limestone runs like a rich, green ribbon from Durness to Assynt, and where wind-blown sand has produced fertile stretches of pasture.

This, then, is the land: often stormy, mountainous, yet rich and fruitful in the hands of its people. Who are they? What is their story? It is a long one and, although archaeological discoveries are made almost every year, much of it has been lost. As we travel, we shall hear episodes from this saga, but a brief outline of the story will provide pegs on which to hang events connected with particular places.

The earliest inhabitants were hunters and gatherers who moved north in small groups in the mesolithic period, around 7000 BC. They left traces of their presence in middens of refuse on some sandy beaches. They were succeeded about 5000 BC by neolithic farming people who tilled the flat land around the coasts and in some straths, and cleared woodland with stone tools. We have evidence of their way of life from tombs of various kinds – chambered cairns, long cairns and passage graves. It is thought that by about 2000 BC a knowledge of metal-working had reached Scotland, marking the start of the Bronze Age. A collection of bronze axe heads found at Migdale belongs to this period. By 500 BC, iron-smelting was widespread.

The north appears on the pages of written history at the time of the Roman occupation of southern Britain. Apart from at least one sea voyage, described in a contemporary account of Agricola's campaigns of conquest in AD 84, the Romans seem never to have shown much interest in Caithness and Sutherland, although pieces of pottery of Roman origin have been found in Caithness brochs. Ptolemy, the Sicilian geographer, listed in the second century AD ten tribes in the Highlands, placing four in the north: the Lugi in south-east Sutherland, the Smertae along the north coast, the Cornovii in Caithness, and the Caereni in the west. Some scholars think that these names might refer to the cults the tribes professed, the Cornovii worshipping the stag or a stag-god, the Caereni being the people of the sheep, but this is speculation, reasonable though it sounds.

In AD 297 we come across for the first time the Picts, listed with others in a Roman document as the enemies of the southern

British. We know tantalizingly little about the Picts. They were
Celts, speaking either a pre-Indo-European tongue or a form of
Celtic akin to Welsh, and they were superb sculptors. They left
us a marvellous legacy of carved stones, decorated with symbols
drawn from life and the imagination. Examples of Pictish stones
are on display in a number of museums: there are some splendid
specimens in the museum at Dunrobin Castle. The meaning of
the Pictish symbols – the crescent, the broken arrow and the
circles and whorls – can only be guessed at. The few lexical
inscriptions have still to be deciphered. For example, the
Ackergill stone, now in the National Museum of Antiquities in
Edinburgh, shows a fish, a rectangle filled with whorls, and a
broken, incomplete inscription in ogam that reads 'Nehtetri'.
But who or what was Nehtetri? Archaeologists still dream of
finding a Rosetta stone that would provide the key to these and
other words.

To spice the mystery, the Picts disappear from the historical
record in the middle of the ninth century. By this time they were
a Christian people, converted by the ministry of St Columba and
other missionaries. It is certain that they intermarried and were
gradually absorbed into the social structure of the invading Scots
from Ireland and, in Caithness and Sutherland, the Norse, but
exactly how this happened is a mystery.

The Norse came in the ninth century, probably first as raiders
and then as settlers. To them we owe much of the present
character of the two counties, including their names.

The Norsemen called the country opposite Orkney 'Katanes',
perhaps deriving the name from an existing local one. 'Katanes'
means 'the headland of the Cat people', and a clue to the origin
of the name lies in the twelfth century document *De Situ
Albanie*, which relates how the first king of the Picts divided
Scotland between his seven sons, one of whom was named Caitt.
Caitt's land, Katanes, Caithness – the derivation is tempting,
but probably wrong. *De Situ Albanie* also says: 'The mountain
of the Mound divides Caithness through the middle.' Taking the
Mound to be the Ord would mean that Caitt, if he existed, ruled
most of the two counties. The Gaelic name for Sutherland is
'Cataibh', meaning 'the land or place of the Cat people'; the
Gaelic for Caithness is 'Gallaibh', 'the place of the foreigners',
the Norsemen presumably.

To the Norse, the east coast south of the Ord was 'the south land', Sutherland. For a long time the name referred only to the east coast; the north-western area was called 'Strathnavern' or 'Strathnaver' or, in Gaelic, 'Duthaich Mhic Aoidh' – 'the land of Mackay'. 'Naver' itself is a very old name, perhaps pre-Indo-European, and may have been the Nabaros referred to by Ptolemy.

The Norse period lasted until the early thirteenth century, by which time the encroaching power of the Scots kings had confined the earldom of Orkney to the northern islands. The four centuries of Norse rule are vividly chronicled in the *Orkneyinga Saga*, the only Icelandic saga to deal extensively with a part of Scotland, and a document that makes this part of our history better known than almost all that happened before and much since. The Norse settlement was concentrated in the north-eastern corner, creating the division in culture and speech that still distinguishes much of Caithness. In fact, Caithness has closer links with Orkney and Shetland than with the Highlands to the south.

With the decline of Norse power came the rise of the clans. The Murrays, Gunns, Mackays and Sinclairs and all the other families whose exploits ring through the succeeding history of the two counties step onto the stage between 1150 and 1350. From the Middle Ages to the eighteenth century, Caithness and Sutherland were scarred by feuds between clans and factions, each struggling to hold its territory and maintain its influence. This was also the time of the *creachadairean*, the caterans, the plunderers, who made a life's work of pillaging their neighbours.

More significantly, this period is also marked by a gradual drawing of Caithness and Sutherland into the mainstream of Scottish affairs. Although the remoteness of the north and the difficulties of travel ensured that the majority of the people remained only partly influenced by distant events, such watersheds in the nation's history as the Reformation and the Act of Union had their effect.

The last Jacobite rising in 1745–6 brought the curtain down on the clans, and during the late-eighteenth and nineteenth centuries life changed in Caithness and Sutherland at a pace and to an extent previously undreamed of. This was the time of the improvers, of the building of roads and harbours, of the growth of the herring fisheries, and of the Clearances. The Clearances were, in a sense, the rump of a revolution in agriculture that had already occurred elsewhere in Europe, a revolution in which the old quasi-feudal order of things was swept away. Peasants were evicted in many countries: in England the enclosure of agricultural land drove many into the cities, where the mills, foundries and factories swallowed them up and turned them into an industrial proletariat. In the Highlands, the Clearances are remembered as a time of suffering and cruelty that emptied the land of its people.

In the next chapter we shall reach some important sites associated with these events and return then to the story. Now, however, it is time to leave Struie Hill and start travelling.

2

Kincardine and Strath Oykel

From the Struie viewpoint, the A836 runs quickly downhill to the south shore of the Dornoch Firth, rejoining the A9, the main north road, almost at sea-level. We are still in Easter Ross at this point, but a little to the west we enter the District of Sutherland. Two signs mark the boundary but it is a spot with little to distinguish it except that the road changes colour in Sutherland to a paler grey. The A9 is rather narrow here, winding between mossy, overgrown dykes and bordered by woods. Formerly the boundary of Sutherland was the Kyle, which we shall presently cross to reach Bonar Bridge, but in the local government reorganization in 1975 the Ross-shire parish of Kincardine was added to the District.

The name Kincardine is derived in part from *carden*, a Pictish word meaning 'thicket'. The small village with this name lies just over a mile inside the eastern boundary of the parish, where the burn Allt Eiteachan spills down to form a small delta in the Firth. Kincardine graveyard is on the south side of the road. The church, with the date 1799 above the door, is abandoned and derelict but the cemetery is still in use. Some of the older tombstones bear the characteristic symbols of death of the eighteenth century – skulls and crossbones, and hour-glasses – and the family crests of those buried there.

After another mile or so, we reach the crossroads village of Ardgay, an important stopping place on the A9 for lorries and buses. Opposite the Lady Ross Hotel sits a white boulder – the Clach Eiteag. The plaque on the plinth tells how the stone used to be carried from parish to parish until by the eighteenth century it marked the site of the local market, the Feill Eiteachan, held in Kincardine every November. The main road turns north here across the Kyle, but before following it we take the road that winds up Strath Carron to Croick.

The strath of the River Carron is about nine miles in length, a broad slice through the hills, marked on both banks by a string of farms. It is a lovely valley, well wooded in the lower part but open to the sky and providing distant views higher up. At Gledfield the river is crossed by a high, arched bridge, from whose south end a footpath leads west to an old mill and on past Gledfield House. On the north bank, where rock outcrops slope steeply to the river, the footpath is carried for part of the way on wooden platforms projecting over the water.

Close to the farm of Gruinards, or Greenyards, on the south bank of the Carron, an important incident in the Clearances occurred in 1854 ...

Much has been written about the Highland clans of Scotland, a good deal of it coloured with a romanticism that hides the truth. Until the early decades of the nineteenth century, the Highlands and its inhabitants were regarded in a negative light by southerners. The country had hardly any roads, and the people were seen as barbaric, primitive, uncouth, violent and a threat to national security. They spoke Gaelic, which, despite once having been the common tongue of most of Scotland, was now incomprehensible to lowlanders.

Land in the Highlands was held by chiefs whose rule was virtually absolute, and towards whom the clan entertained an almost fanatical loyalty. The chiefs leased large tracts of land to tacksmen, often their relatives, who in turn rented land to tenants and cottars. The latter two groups paid rent in money but more often in labour and goods to the tacksman, who in turn paid his rent usually in cash to the chief. In the early eighteenth century the economy was pastoral, based on the herding and rearing of black cattle, although oats, barley and vegetables were grown and along the coasts some fishing was carried on. Subsistence agriculture was the way of life of most of the people: poverty was widespread and famine was not unknown. But, although the material comfort of the clansfolk was bereft of much, they remained a people of spirit, with a rich folk culture that often touched high levels of expression. From illiterate parishioners in Kildonan, between 1787 and 1824, the Reverend Alexander Sage collected heroic ballads, some of which were published in 1892 in an anthology called *Reliquiae Celticae*.

The chiefs seemed to be forever engaged in struggles with their neighbours over land. Lawsuits and cattle-raiding sometimes spilled into open blood feuds, and then the chief called upon all his tenants to bear arms in his support. This was the system that Charles Edward Stuart exploited in 1745 to raise an army to drive the House of Hanover from the throne of Britain, and the system that was brought to the concluding chapter of its history amid the rain and heather on Culloden Moor in April 1746. After the defeat of the Jacobites, government troops occupied the Highlands to ensure that never again would the Gaelic-speaking northerners be a threat. In fact, the people of Caithness and Sutherland had remained largely loyal to the Hanoverian regime during the rebellion but they suffered in the aftermath along with the others.

Towards the end of the eighteenth century the economy of the Highlands fell into serious trouble. The trade in black cattle declined. The clan chiefs and their families had begun to spend a great deal of time and money in the salons of Edinburgh and London and were finding the income from their lands insufficient to support an often profligate life-style. The chiefs became the first to cast off the obligations of the clan society: they no longer needed large bodies of tenants to provide ready armies and enhance their status. The old system of land in exchange for arms was gone. But as the chiefs shed their traditional roles, their people still clung to the old ways, tilling their plots of ground by primitive means, secure in their belief in traditional rights that had no basis in the recognized laws of property.

The chiefs began to look for ways of improving their incomes. At the same time, a population increase took place in the Highlands: the squeeze on the land's productivity went unnoticed for a long time, as people divided their tenancies into smaller holdings, broke in more moorland and began to cultivate the new potato. Towards the end of the century, however, famine struck.

'The poor, who cannot afford to buy, are in a miserable situation,' wrote John Bethune, the minister of Dornoch, in the

1790s. 'To meliorate the condition at once of the land and of the tenants, it is evident, that such very small possessions as many of them have, should not be permitted to exist. In the present state of the country, they [the tenancies] would not furnish a comfortable subsistence, if they had them for nothing.' Bethune's words were echoed by commentators in other areas. The minister of Tongue wrote: 'Not only the poor ... but families of many small farmers were reduced to the most deplorable situation for want of bread.' Andrew Gallie found that many of his parishioners in Kincardine 'were reduced to poverty by the loss of their cattle, and the almost total failure of the crop ... which occasioned such distress, that they were obliged to remove with their families, and settle in the low country [Easter Ross], as day labourers or domestic servants'. He thought that the population had dropped by almost one quarter.

The heritors, as the landowners were called at the time, spent considerable sums on meal and other victuals to avert catastrophe, and it seems from contemporary accounts that no one actually starved to death. Famine relief was, of course, a further drain on the landlords' resources, and one that they could not hope to recoup from the low rents their tenants could afford to pay. Sir John Lockhart-Ross had sent pease, barley, flour and potatoes to relieve hunger and 'had discounted one third of the arrears of rent, over the whole of his estate'.

In 1762 Sir John Lockhart-Ross had fallen heir to the large estate of Balnagowan, which extended from the Dornoch Firth to the head of Strath Oykel and included most of the parish of Kincardine. Ross had recently given up a successful career in the navy, and now he turned to agriculture with enthusiasm and a passion for reform. He introduced new crops, reclaimed fields, drained marshland and became the first man to introduce sheep-farming on a new commercial scale to the north. Sheep-farmers were already leasing large tracts of ground in Perth and Argyll to graze the hardy, black-faced Linton sheep. Of course, sheep were already common in the Highlands but they were kept in small numbers to supply their owners with wool, milk and mutton, and the local breeds were taken indoors every night to protect them from the weather. Cattle were the favoured animals of the tenantry, who looked with scorn at the new sheep and were convinced that they would not outlast the winter. But

Lockhart-Ross's Lintons thrived at Balnagowan, and in 1782 he leased part of his estate to Thomas Geddes from Tummel Bridge, probably the first lowland sheep-farmer to move beyond the Great Glen.

In 1788 the estate of Rosehall in the parish of Creich, north of Kincardine, was consolidated into one large sheep-run. More and more the landowners turned to sheep as the answer to their problems of falling income and in the belief that they were 'improving' the economy. During the four decades after 1770, the price of wool rose to high levels, and it became very profitable to lease land to enterprising southern sheep-farmers instead of to tenants working an old-fashioned agriculture.

Cheviot sheep, introduced to the north in 1790 by Sir John Sinclair of Ulbster, were tougher even than the Lintons, and they survived where deer and black cattle failed. The tenants suddenly found themselves unwanted, in the way of the sheep, the old clan ties of loyalty and chiefly obligation obsolete.

On the Balnagowan estate, however, there was resistance. Thomas Geddes found some of his Lintons being shot or driven into lochs to drown. To the south of Kincardine, in Strath Rusdale, the tenants who had been displaced to make room for sheep found themselves having to pay fines to the sheep-farmers to redeem cattle that had strayed onto the new farms. At this time the land was largely unenclosed and animals wandered unhindered across the unfenced braes. Eventually, fed up with the humiliation of paying fines to get back their own animals, the small tenants of Strath Rusdale decided to release some penned-up cattle by force. This took place in the early summer of 1792 – a year afterwards to be remembered in Gaelic as *Bliadhna nan Caoraich*, 'the year of the sheep'. In the course of the freeing of the cattle, some shepherds claimed that they were beaten up, and one of the farmers was forcibly disarmed when he pulled a pistol on the tenants. This skirmish set panic rushing through the authorities. The landowners banded together, and rumours of revolt swept the countryside (the French Revolution had rocked Europe only three years before). While the authorities mustered to quell what they saw as the beginning of a rebellion, the Strath Rusdale men went cheerfully to a wedding to celebrate a blow struck against the loathed southerners and their sheep. Encouraged by their success in releasing their captured cattle, the men decided to drive every last Cheviot and Linton from Strath Carron and Strath Oykel to the Beauly Firth and beyond. On Sunday 29 July the word went around the townships from house to kirk door to house to gather for this ridding of an evil from their midst.

We do not know how many men took part: the Sheriff of Tain estimated four hundred, but he may have been exaggerating for political reasons of his own. On the last day of July, the drovers gathered in Strath Oykel and went up to Lairg. Here they collected the sheep into large flocks and drove them down Achany Glen to Invershin and across the Kyle, reaching Boath in Easter Ross by Friday 5 of August.

In response to the anxious appeals of the landowners, three companies of the 42nd Regiment had marched from Fort George outside Inverness. On the afternoon of the 6th, the troops reached Dingwall, where they paraded and then set off with the assembled landowners to confront the 'rebels'. When the troops came up to Boath, the sheep-drovers scattered to their homes without offering any resistance. The authorities congratulated themselves on having snuffed out an insurrection, although there was no intention on the part of the drovers to challenge political authority.

A few men were hunted down and taken to Inverness to stand trial, charged with various offences including instigating a riot and seizing sheep unlawfully. Five men, four of them from Kincardine parish and the other from Alness, were found guilty. Malcolm Ross was fined £50, an impossible sum for a tenant to meet, and sentenced to jail until it was paid; Donald Munro and Alexander Mackay were banished for life; William Cunningham received a prison sentence of three months, and Hugh Breac Mackenzie, the Alness man, was sentenced to be transported to Botany Bay for seven years. However, all five escaped mysteriously one night from the jail in Inverness and were never heard of again.

From the beginning of the nineteenth century the eviction of tenants increased, but Strath Carron itself was not 'cleared' until 1854. By this time, popular feeling had been aroused against the action of the landowners. In several parts of the Highlands, tenants had banded together and successfully resisted eviction. Newspapers were carrying accounts of the more sensational clearances, and the landlords were growing conscious of their public image. Writers such as Donald Ross, a Glasgow lawyer, produced articles and pamphlets strongly attacking the lairds; Ross was a witness to the Strath Carron evictions.

In a cold, grey dawn at the end of March, the Sheriff-Substitute of Tain and a party of about thirty-five men, including police from Dingwall and Inverness, arrived in the strath to enforce the notices to quit that had been served on the tenants some time before. They had been expected, and a crowd gathered to resist them. As frequently happened, the women of the strath stood in front, to oppose the police, while the men stayed behind. The tenants armed themselves with sticks and refused to allow the Sheriff's party to carry out their orders to clear the houses. After attempts to dissuade the tenants from impeding them, the police attacked with a baton charge. Donald Ross described the mayhem that ensued: '... more than twenty females were carried off the field in blankets and litters; and the appearance they presented, with their heads cut and bruised, their limbs mangled, and their clothes clotted with blood, was such as would horrify any savage.' It was said that the grass and the earth were dyed red with blood and that the dogs came to lick it up.

The brutality of the police caused a furore in the press. The Lord Advocate of Scotland demanded an explanation from the Sheriff of Tain. Official reports of the event are, predictably perhaps, less sensational than those written by Donald Ross but they concede that police inflicted severe injuries on the women. In the long run, however, the law remained the law, and in the following year the tenants of Strath Carron were evicted without further resistance.

In little over a decade, the strath's population of perhaps five hundred was reduced almost to nothing. A sad reminder of the evictions is to be found scratched on the windows of the little church at Croick, near the head of the strath where Glencalvie and Strath Cuileannach meet.

The church was built by Thomas Telford in 1827. At the time of the evictions the minister was Gustavus Aird, twenty-eight years old, respected and trusted by his parishioners. When the Glencalvie folk received notices to quit, they appealed to Aird for his help, but like many ministers of that time he recognized that the people had to obey the law, however odious and unjust it might appear. He wrote to the factor of the estate to put the tenants' case, offered his manse at Bonar Bridge as accommodation for those campaigning against the eviction, and set himself up to receive food or money on their behalf. 'Matters have really come to an awful pitch,' he wrote, 'when beings possessed of immortal souls, originally created after the divine image, are driven out of their homes and fatherland to make way for fir and larch plants, deer, roes, moorgame, partridges and hares.' His efforts were in vain. Immortal souls counted for nothing against bank balances. The evictions took place in 1845. With nowhere to go, their spirits at a low ebb, the people sheltered in the churchyard among the gravestones of their ancestors. On the outside of the east window they scratched the record of their passing: 'Glencalvie people was in the churchyard here May 24 1845 ... Glencalvie people the wicked generation ... Glencalvie is a wilderness blow ship them to the colony ....' They wrote in English, as if recognizing that there would be few around to read a valediction in Gaelic.

The church at Croick is still used for worship in the summer months. The messages on the window are protected by sheets of glass. When I went there to take photographs for this book, I met a woman who had been christened there in 1909: she could not remember what the church had been like then, for she had emigrated with her family when she was two years old. The interior of the church is plain, as are many Highland churches, with white walls and darkly varnished pews. Conifers, chestnut and ash trees flourish in the graveyard and form a little patch of woodland in an otherwise treeless glen. The hills around are speckled brown and green, a reminder that until the Clearances they had long been subject to cultivation. For thousands of years, in fact, for outside the churchyard wall above the burn are the roots of a broch dating from around the time of Christ.

The population of sheep in Sutherland rose from about 5,000 in 1808 to 168,000 in 1853. Since then it has fallen to less than 100,000, but the glens remain empty.

Beyond Amat Lodge, at the mouth of Glencalvie, on flat land in a loop of the river, is a pink obelisk, protected by an iron railing. This is the burial place of a chief of Clan Ross, George Ross of

Pitcalnie, who died in 1884, and his wife, Catherine Gilchrist of Ospisdale.

Further up the glen, at Glencalvie Lodge, the road divides. Glencalvie itself leads south to Diebidale Lodge and Glen Diebidale under the flank of Carn Chuinneag. The main glen of the Carron runs west for 1½ miles to split again close to Alladale Lodge into two long glens that trend south-westwards. Gleann Mor, the longer of the two, is nearly six miles from the Carron to where it merges into Gleann Beag at Deanich Lodge. This is the southern boundary of the parish of Kincardine and of Sutherland District.

The other glen that leads up from Alladale Lodge carries the Alladale river and ends beneath the mountain called Bodach Beag, 'the little old man'. All of this vast area, and the moors and streams of the Freevater Forest, must be explored on foot and by properly equipped walkers. Steep, rocky corries form a rampart along the north slope of Bodach Beag and the ridge of high ground, with the summits of Carn Ban and Seana Bhraigh, running west from it. Seana Bhraigh, at 2,972 feet, just falls short of being a Munro.

From Croick a track runs up Strath Cuileannach and continues as a footpath over the moors to Glen Einig. The river that drains the strath, 'the Black Water' in English, makes a great westward sweep from the head of the strath and as the Glasha Burn leads to a corrie between Bodach Beag and Carn Ban. From Glen Einig, the nine miles of Strath Mulzie run south and then south-east to Coire Mor, the 'great corrie', on the west flank of Carn Ban.

The boundary of Sutherland District follows Gleann Beag to the ridge above the corrie of Cadha Dearg, and then along the upper part of the River Douchary for nearly three miles until it turns sharply east and climbs to the col south of the summit of Meall nam Bradhan. The boundary passes along the summit ridge to the north to the head of the main stretch of Strath Mulzie, zigzags along Allt nan Caorach and around Loch an Daimh, and then runs north-eastwards along Druim nan Feannag to the Rappach Water, where it turns westwards again before veering north to the summit of Meall an Fhuarain. From here it runs west, on the map stitching the tops along the ridge of the Cromalt Hills to the A835 just to the south of Elphin. The boundary then follows the course of the lower part of the Abhainn a'Chnocain to Loch Veyatie, whence it passes along the Fionn Loch and down the valley of the Kirkaig River to the sea.

The broad waters of the Kyle of Sutherland mark the original boundary of the county. Along the south shore of the Kyle, the road leads past Invercharron House and Invercharron Mains down on the flat, fertile delta of the Carron. From here to the little station at Culrain the road runs parallel to the railway line.

Until the viaduct at Culrain and the road bridge at Bonar were built, the only way to cross the Kyle dryshod was by boat. Andrew Gallie listed five ferries in operation in the 1790s: at Bonar, Invercharron, Culrain, Tighniriver and Ochtow. Cattle-drovers swam their animals across, the readiness with which a beast took to the water being interpreted as a forecast of the price it would fetch at the tryst; when one refused altogether to swim, it had to be ferried across in a coble.

By June 1864 the railway line had reached Tain in Ross-shire, and by October the station at Ardgay. In the following year, the Sutherland Railway Company was formed and work began to extend the line. It took nearly three years to complete the thirty-six miles to Golspie: the Kyle was bridged by the expensive viaduct at Culrain, five stone arches and a girder span of 230 feet, and extensive rock cuttings had to be blasted or hacked out to make a way up Achany Glen to Lairg. The major shareholder in the Sutherland Railway Company and the chairman of its board was the third Duke of Sutherland. He hoped that by building the line via Lairg instead of along the more obvious coastal route the isolated expanse of north-west Sutherland would be opened to development.

There was no station at Culrain until 1871, when one was opened in response to the complaints of travellers who until then had to journey to Ardgay to catch the train. Until January 1917 the short trip across the viaduct from Culrain to Invershin cost one halfpenny, the cheapest third-class single ticket available anywhere in the country. Now both Culrain and Invershin are request stops.

The mansion of Carbisdale Castle occupies a commanding site on a rocky spur overlooking the Kyle. Scotland's most recent 'castle', it came to be built through an extravagant fit of family spite. In November 1888 Anne Hay-Mackenzie, the Countess of

Cromarty, died. She and her husband, the third Duke of Sutherland, were already estranged but when the Duke remarried only three months later, his family were shocked. His new wife was Mary Blair, the widow of an Indian Civil Servant; he revised his will in her favour and when he expired from a burst duodenal ulcer in 1892, almost all his personal fortune, nearly £1,400,000, went to her. His son Cromartie disputed the will, and the contest between him and his stepmother, the Dowager Duchess, became so acrimonious that at one point Mary was found guilty of contempt of court, fined £250 and sent to Holloway prison for forty days. The contest was eventually settled, but in 1896 Mary married again – her new spouse was Sir Albert Rollitt MP – and decided to build a castle to rival the Sutherland seat at Dunrobin. Unable to obtain a site in Sutherland, where almost all the land belonged to her stepson, she chose Carbisdale. The construction of the castle began in 1906 and continued until about 1914, two years after Mary's death. It is said that when the Duke of Sutherland rolled past Carbisdale in his private train, he drew the blinds so as not to see the fine masonry on the rock above the Kyle.

In the 1930s the castle was bought by the Salvesens, a wealthy whaling-shipping family. In 1943 it passed to Captain Harold Salvesen, who tried in vain to sell it, considered giving it away to be an old folks' home but eventually gifted it and its farm and woodlands to the Scottish Youth Hostels Association. Carbisdale is now the largest youth hostel in Britain, with 250 beds, and also the most well appointed, considering the paintings, antique furniture and a ballroom resplendent with white classical statuary. The walls of the castle are built from local whinstone with freestone additions. The grand staircase is copied from one in an Essex manor-house by Grinling Gibbons, a seventeenth-century woodcarver. Four stained-glass windows above the stair depict the steady rise through the ranks of the British nobility of the ancestors of the Dukes of Sutherland.

The flat land to the south of the castle is the site of the battle in April 1650 when the Marquis of Montrose was defeated by government troops. It is sometimes given the name of the nearby rocky hill, Creag a' Choineachan – 'the hill of lamentation'.

The Marquis was marching south at the head of an army of Danes, Germans and Orkneymen, in support of the exiled

Charles II. A little over a year before, Scotland had declared Charles her king but he, mindful perhaps of the fate that had befallen his father in Whitehall, was biding his time in Europe. Montrose's courageous bid to rouse the country for the King ended on the braes of Carbisdale. Anticipating his moves, a troop of cavalry under the command of Lieutenant-Colonel Strachan met his army near the mouth of the Carron. Strachan's force was in three columns: the first was thrown back by Montrose's men, but when Strachan led the second column in a charge, the Marquis's soldiers turned and fled. Most of them were either killed or taken prisoner. Montrose's flag was found in the heather with his cloak, his sword and the star of the Order of the Garter. He himself had escaped westward to Assynt disguised as a commoner. What befell him there we shall tell later.

A minor road follows the south shore of the Kyle beyond Culrain as far as Langwell, where a little bridge spans the river to connect with the main Strath Oykel road. Close to here, where the river doglegs through a narrow cleft, are the ruins of a dun, an ancient fortress dating probably from the Iron Age.

To take the main road up Strath Oykel, the A836, it is necessary to cross the Kyle at Bonar Bridge.

Bonar is a pleasant village, its shops, houses and hotels spread in a line along the road. The name is most likely a derivation from the Gaelic *bonnath*, 'bottom ford'; in a document written in 1566, it is referred to as Bonach. The present bridge, a handsome coathanger-shaped structure, leads right into the centre of the village and is the third on the site. A stone triangular monument at the north end provides a potted history of this important crossing, the main route into Sutherland, with elevation drawings of each of the three bridges. 'Traveller', commands the inscription, 'STOP and read with gratitude the names of the Parliamentary Commissioners appointed in 1803, to direct the making of above Five Hundred miles of Roads through the Highlands of Scotland and of numerous Bridges....'

Before the nineteenth century Sutherland could boast of only one bridge, at Brora. There were no roads deserving the name, and in Caithness and Sutherland carts were almost unknown. Goods were carried on people's backs or by long trains of packhorses. Livestock was driven on the hoof. The mail service was staffed by runners: in 1802 the carrying of the post from Tain to Caithness was increased from three journeys a week to daily. The postal rates then were about 3d for a distance of up to fifty miles, and 6d for a delivery of over 150 miles – very expensive in relation to the wages of the time.

The first bridge at Bonar was built under the direction of Thomas Telford. This man's name crops up again and again in the history of the north. Born in Eskdale in 1757, the son of a shepherd, this remarkable civil engineer built over nine hundred miles of road in the Highlands as well as bridges, churches and manses. His other achievements include the Caledonian Canal and the Menai Bridge, and the Swedish government knighted him for his work in laying out the Gota Canal.

Between 1809 and 1819, roads were driven through Caithness and Sutherland by Telford and his colleagues. In 1819 the first coach ran from Inverness to Thurso; carrying three passengers inside and three on top, it left Inverness at six in the morning and, travelling at six miles per hour, reached Thurso at 7.30 on the following morning. Some parts of Sutherland did not receive a mail service until much later: in 1828 a runner enjoying an annual salary of £20 began deliveries between Bonar and Assynt. By 1859 Caithness had 231 miles of road and Sutherland 510. There were several tolls in Caithness but none in Sutherland, although travellers had to pay to use the several ferries. Some of the tollhouses can still be seen, for example at Thurso. A man is recorded as saying that the new road (now the A9) 'created a new epoch' in the history of the north.

Telford's bridge at Bonar was cast in Denbighshire and transported north in pieces to be assembled *in situ*. The cost was over £13,000; work began in June 1811 and was finished in November 1812. The bridge had three arches, two of stone and one of iron, with a span of 150 feet.

On a Friday afternoon in February 1892, a rampaging flood of ice and meltwater dealt Telford's bridge its death blow. Loud cracks warned of the impending collapse, and a witness wrote that it was 'lifted by the current from its foundation, and dashed to the bottom of the channel, where it lies in shattered fragments completely out of sight'. The flood engulfed the whole breadth of the Kyle, submerging farms and homes, sweeping away boats and livestock, but the destruction of the bridge was 'the greatest blow of all'. The Ross and Sutherland county councils lost no

The Beauly Firth from Struie Hill.

The church window at Croick where evicted tenants
scratched messages in 1845.

Croick church is still used in the summer months.

The bridge at Bonar Bridge is the third on the site, but the earlier two are remembered on the monument in the foreground.

Carbisdale Castle dominates the woods along the Kyle of Sutherland.

Shin Falls.

Strath Oykel: the Tutim burn descends by the houses on the left, and the battle, An Là Tuiteam Tarbhach, may have been fought in this vicinity.

This standing stone, twice the height of a person, is right beside the A9 between Spinningdale and Ospisdale.

Dornoch Cathedral.

The rallying stone of Clan Sutherland on the old bridge at Golspie.

Dunrobin Castle.

Helmsdale.

Navidale, with the hills beyond rising towards the Ord of Caithness.

Some of the stones comprising the stone circle at Achavanich.

time in building a new bridge, and it opened, three arches of cantilevered iron, in July 1893. This bridge lasted until 1973, when it was replaced by the existing one.

Like almost all the villages along the east coast of Sutherland, Bonar did not develop until the early decades of the nineteenth century. By 1834 boats of up to sixty tons were trading from here, importing meal, coal and lime and exporting fir props, wool, oak-bark, corn and salmon. George Dempster, the proprietor, was offering plots of land to tenants. There was an inn, and cattle-markets were held in July, August and September. It is worth pausing in Bonar, to stroll along the main street above the river. In summer salmon-fishermen dragnet in the Kyle where the delta of the Carron pushes the south shore almost to the north bank. From the war memorial there is a good view of the wide carseland, and nearby, on the wall of a weaving shop, is a statue of a MacGregor clansman based on a nineteenth-century MacIan print.

The A836 runs along the north shore of the Kyle past the Invershin Hotel and under the Culrain viaduct. The site of Invershin Castle is an airy, wooded mound beside the river. There is hardly any visible trace of the castle, but dense thickets of nettles show where it stood, and the lines of walls and ditches are evident in the grass. Just beyond the castle site, the Strath Oykel road, the A837, forks off to the left to cross the Shin beside Inveran power station. Keeping to the edge of the hillside on the north of the river Oykel, the road skirts the flood plain of this broad waterway for a few miles until it nears Rosehall, where it rises away from the river. Just before Rosehall stand two churches: the second, the Free Church, has a curious octagonal porch. Then, at the junction of the A837 and the A389 to Lairg, we come upon the local war memorial. The traveller will find these all over the north, sometimes in the centre of a village, sometimes on an isolated braeside. The Rosehall example is a Celtic cross, a common design; others are abstract obelisks or bear representations of soldiers.

After another mile or so, we reach the mouth of Glencassley. The glen cuts north through the hills and is serviced by a single-track road for most of its fifteen-mile length. After the road gives out, a track continues up to a clutch of bogs and small lochs on the northern side of Ben More Assynt. A short distance from the mouth of the glen, the Cassley Falls present a fine combination of forest, rock and burn, where the water has cut across the grain of the rocks to leave the eroded strata sticking up like miniature mountain ranges.

After the Cassley the next main burn to join the Oykel is the Tutim. It tumbles down through a narrow cleft to the flat floor of the strath. Here the Oykel meanders through broad beds of shingle flanked by meadows, and it was somewhere here that in 1406 a battle was fought between the Macleods and the Mackays. It is known as An Là Tuiteam Tarbhach – 'the day of the great slaughter'. There was at the time a dispute between Hugh Mackay, the brother of the late chief of the clan, and his sister-in-law, the chief's widow. She complained to her brother, Malcolm Macleod of Lewis, and he hastened with an armed force to her aid. Nothing was resolved apparently and the Macleods left, but not before helping themselves to Mackay cattle. Hugh pursued them and caught up with them in Strath Oykel: in the ensuing conflict it is said that all the Macleods fell except one, who escaped to tell the tale.

Probably the southern boundary of the province of Kat in ancient times, Strath Oykel is a major route through to the west coast. Up until the time of the Clearances it was well populated but now you can drive the length of the road and pass only a few houses.

As we travel west, the country rises and becomes more open and wild, resounding in the spring to the cries of the curlew and the lapwing. But suddenly, at Oykel Bridge, the road drops to cross the river: here, like an oasis, the Oykel Bridge Hotel sits. The old bridge is closed to traffic but it is wise to stop and walk across it to see the gorge of the river just upsteam. Now on the west bank of the Oykel, the road continues its ascent to the spine of the country. The watershed is reached at Cnoc Chaornaidh: rain falling on the east side of this prominent bald hump runs to the Dornoch Firth, that falling on the west feeds the burns racing to the Atlantic. In this area there are the remains of several chambered cairns of neolithic age.

Further to the west is the Altnacealgach Hotel. The name is Gaelic for 'burn of the deceivers' and gives some substance to the old story that, in a dispute over the Ross-shire boundary, a Ross-shire man filled his shoes with earth from his home so that no matter where he stood he could truthfully claim to be on Ross-shire soil. Before the 1975 District boundary changes, a piece of Ross-shire ran north like a horn into Sutherland, to the summit of Ben More Assynt. The Altnacealgach Hotel is also the boundary of Assynt, to which we shall come back in the last chapter of this book. Now it is time to return to Bonar to pick up the A9 again.

3

The Dornoch Peninsula and Lairg

On the way east from Bonar, the A9 runs along the shore of the Firth, slanting across wooded slopes above the water. After about three miles it passes the high, rounded prominence of Dun Creich. The summit of this hill is wooded but it stands isolated from the neighbouring high land by the low fields of the farm of Creich Mains. Dun Creich is the site of the most northerly vitrified fort in Scotland. These structures date from the Iron Age and get their name from the fact that some of the stones used in their construction have been partly melted and fused by great heat into a glass-like state. This was probably effected by firing the timber lacing in the masonry. The inner and outer ramparts of Dun Creich enclose an area of over 55,000 square feet. It is not hard to imagine its strength in its heyday, on the summit of its hill, unapproachable except from below.

The fort may have more significance. The place-name element 'pit', from the Pictish word *pett*, meaning a share, is considered to mark a place inhabited by Celtic-speaking Picts. There are over three hundred such names in Scotland, but only five in Sutherland and none in Caithness. The Sutherland names are all found in fairly close proximity to Dun Creich. Does this mean that the Dornoch Firth was some kind of frontier between Celtic-speaking and non-Celtic-speaking Picts?

Moving away from Dun Creich, the road curves around the flank of a steep, forested hill to the little village of Spinningdale. Down near the shore, hidden by trees for the most part, stand the gaunt ruins of an old cotton-mill, a reminder of an early attempt to bring industry to the area. The local landowner, George Dempster of Skibo, had David Dale, the leading cotton-manufacturer in the country, erect the mill in 1790 to use the new Lancashire spinning jennies. It once had a hundred employees but distance from urban markets caused it to fail. In 1808 a fire destroyed the building, and it was left in ruins; in 1829 a traveller noted 'the deserted hamlet'.

George Dempster was one of the more enlightened of the improving landlords. He bought Skibo estate in 1786, and he died in 1818 at the age of eighty-six, well liked by his tenants. His ideas for improvement included the granting of life-leases to tenants, a scheme he thought better in the long run than letting the land as sheep runs.

There is an alternative route east from Bonar to Spinningdale through Migdale. It follows a minor road that climbs steeply up through Bonar to open crofting country around Loch Migdale. Bonar golf course is splendidly situated at the west end of this loch, with a splendid view along the water lying in a fold in the hills. A hoard of Bronze Age relics, including an axe, eight armlets, beads and sheets of bronze, an earring and buttons, were found here. In the churchyard of the Free Church at Migdale there is a solitary grave marked by a marble stone: this is the last resting place of the Reverend Gustavus Aird who, says the inscription, 'entered into the joy of his Lord on 20th December 1898'.

From Migdale the road squeezes east through a narrow glen between Migdale Rock and Creag a'Bhealaich to Spinningdale.

At Ospisdale the A9 bends away from the sea. The land flattens out a little, and the fields become larger. Between the road and sea is Skibo Castle, completely shielded from the A9 by its plantations. The castle used to belong to Andrew Carnegie, the American steel magnate. Carnegie was born in Dunfermline but made his vast fortune in America. His income was staggering ($23 million in 1900, for example), and when he bought Skibo he turned it into a lavish baronial mansion, adding an extension larger than the original and laying out a nine-hole golf course in the grounds. He and his family were in the habit of spending four or five months every year at this retreat, entertaining an impressive guest list that included artists, politicians and literati and, on one occasion, King Edward VII. After his death in 1918, his daughter, who at the age of two had laid the foundation stone for the extension, continued the tradition of the summer visit until old age made travelling too difficult for her.

Skibo's history, however, goes back to the Middle Ages, when it was a residence of the bishops of Dornoch. In 1760 a visitor remarked that the garden was very good, producing 'all sorts of fruit in great perfection, and I believe not more than six weeks later than about London'.

To see Skibo, albeit distantly, it is necessary to turn off the A9 at Clashmore and take the minor road that leads down to Meikle Ferry. This was the northern terminus of the main route across the Firth before Telford built his bridge at Bonar. The coast is low and sandy and covered in scrubby vegetation – whins, heather and broom. At Meikle Ferry there is one slipway, divided by a wall, and one house. Opposite, on the Ross-shire side, a long spur of land reaches out into the Firth and was the southern terminus of the ferry. In a tragic accident in August 1809, almost one hundred lives were lost when the boat, overcrowded with folk heading for the Lammas Fair at Tain, capsized. Behind the peninsula at Meikle Ferry lies a broad, shallow lagoon, which empties at low tide to reveal mud flats; the River Evelix wanders lazily across it, and beyond, on the north shore, stands Skibo Castle.

Among the farms that dot the links between Meikle Ferry and Dornoch is one called Cyderhall. The name has nothing to do with fermented apple juice but is a corruption of the Norse for 'Sigurd's Howe', the mound of Sigurd, and marks the spot where, tradition has it, a Norse chieftain was buried in the ninth century. Sigurd received the earldom of Orkney from his brother Rognvald and, in alliance with other Viking noblemen, invaded Caithness. They subdued the country as far south as the Oykel, perhaps in AD 875. Thus Caithness and Sutherland were drawn into the Norse world. There was, however, resistance to this conquest, and one of its leaders was a local *mormaor*, or chief, called Maelbrigte, who was noted for having prominent buck-teeth. In the words of Samuel Laing's translation of the thirteenth-century history *Heimskringla*, Sigurd killed Mael-brigte 'and hung his head to his stirrup leather; but the calf of the leg was scratched by the teeth, which were sticking out from the head, and the wound caused inflammation in his leg, of which the earl died, and he was laid in a mound …'.

With a population of about 850, Dornoch must be a contender for the title of smallest county town in Britain. It is now a quiet place of honey-coloured houses, lanes, wynds and gardens, reached by the A949 which leaves the A9 just after it crosses the Evelix. From Meikle Ferry a minor road leads into the town. The countryside here bears the marks of a long settlement, reaching back into neolithic times, when the coastal links, well drained, must have been attractive to the early farming communities.

In the Middle Ages, Dornoch became a place of great importance as the seat of the bishops of Caithness. Its cathedral, now a kirk of the Church of Scotland, still dominates the town's skyline, the spire on its sturdy tower visible from every quarter. St Finbarr, or Barr, is reputed to have been the first missionary to bring the gospel here, and his chapel is believed to have stood at the eastern corner of the present graveyard. As with most of the saintly men who spread out with staff and Bible from the centres of early Christianity at Lindisfarne and later Iona, not much is known about Finbarr. He may have been a Caithness man and he probably carried on his ministry in the fifth century. Other saints who may have had some association with the area include Duthac, the patron saint of Tain, Donnan, who gave his name to Kildonan, and Maolrubha, after whom Loch Maree is named.

The Celtic church, primarily a monastic institution, was replaced by the hierarchical, parish-based Catholic church in the eleventh and twelfth centuries. Shortly after 1140, David I wrote to the Earl of Orkney telling him, 'As you love me, you shall love the monks that live at Dornoch in Caithness, and their men and property….' Religious centres, with their gold and silver appurtenances and illuminated manuscripts in jewelled bindings, were favourite targets for Viking marauders, and Dornoch was within easy reach of any raiding longship crew from Orkney.

The first bishop of Caithness and Sutherland about whom we know anything was Andrew, appointed about 1153 by David I. It was, however, Gilbert de Moravia, the fourth bishop, who founded the cathedral. He assumed his episcopacy in 1223 and died in 1245 at Scrabster, where he had a palace. Gilbert is remembered as a good preacher and a humane, capable man: he was canonized after his death, and oaths were sworn on his relics until the Reformation swept away the infrastructure of popery. Gilbert modelled the statutes of Dornoch Cathedral on those of Moray, where he had been the archdeacon, and founded several hospices to cater for the poor. A copy of the cathedral charter, dated to about 1224, hangs on the wall of the north transept of the present building and records that, 'In the times before our [Gilbert's] administration there was ... but one priest ... both on account of the poverty of the place and also of frequent invasions.' Gilbert overcame the poverty by ensuring that fourteen parish churches in his diocese contributed to the upkeep of the cathedral; he also laid down rules about how long the ten new canons should remain at Dornoch – for example, the dean 'at least for the half of every year'.

In the nave of the cathedral, a life-size stone figure marks the tomb of Gilbert's brother, Sir Richard de Moravia, who was killed in a battle with the Norse. Most of the detail of his effigy is worn away but we can still distinguish his sword and his surcoat and the little dog crouching in permanent fidelity at his feet. The struggle in which Sir Richard fell may have been the same one in which the town's coat of arms gained its horseshoe. In 1259 an invading force of Norsemen landed at Embo. The defending army was led by William, the first Earl of Sutherland. In the conflict, William lost his sword and grabbed the nearest weapon to hand, a horse's leg, with which he laid about effectively enough to overcome his opponents.

In 1271 a convent of Red Friars was founded at Dornoch but all trace of it has disappeared.

The eighth bishop of Caithness was an Englishman, Alan de St Edmund: his election to office at the end of the thirteenth century indicates the influence of Edward I in Scottish affairs, and in 1291 the English king elevated Alan to the post of Chancellor of Scotland. By 1310, however, the winds of political change had blasted through the country: the bishop was Ferquherd, who acknowledged Robert Bruce as king.

In 1570 Dornoch was besieged by the combined forces of George Sinclair, Earl of Caithness, and the Chief of Clan Mackay. Three years before, the Earl of Sutherland and his wife had been poisoned at Helmsdale. Although Sinclair was suspected of being behind this murder, he became the guardian of the Earl's son, then only fifteen years old. Sinclair, a canny rogue whom we shall meet again, brought his ward to Girnigoe Castle near Wick and married him to his daughter Barbara, who was nearly twice his age. Only after this union did Sinclair allow the young Master of Sutherland to return to his family home at Dunrobin. However, this was not the end of the story.

The Murray family of Dornoch were enemies of Sinclair. Suspecting him of plotting to place his own son in the earldom of Sutherland, they persuaded the Master of Sutherland to flee from Dunrobin to safety in Aberdeen. Sinclair responded by marching on Dornoch, and Iye Dhu Mackay, the thirteenth chief of his clan, was more than willing to join the expedition for another round in a feud that had persisted for decades. At the time Dornoch was a small place – a collection of cottages and lanes clustered about the cathedral. The attackers fought their way into the vennel on the north side of the cathedral, forcing the defenders to retreat to the castle and the steeple. Sinclair's men set fire to everything that would burn and lifted everything worth taking; William Sutherland of Evelix, one of Sinclair's officers, is said to have kicked open the tomb of Bishop Gilbert in his search for loot, and the story goes that he later contracted a terrible, fatal disease in the offending foot.

The Murrays held out for a week and then negotiated a surrender. Three of their men were delivered as hostages. Sinclair wanted to execute them at once, but his son and Iye Dhu objected to this breach of the rules of war, a stand that was later to cost one of them his life. Sinclair's son-in-law, the Laird of Duffus, had no such scruples and he despatched the hostages.

The destruction of the cathedral occasioned in this affray coincided with the Reformation. For many years the part-ruin continued to serve as a parish church until, on the night of 5 November 1605, it was further damaged by a great storm: 'The inner stone pillars of the north syd ... laiking the roof befor, were blown from the very roots quyt clein over the outer walles of the church; which walles did remain nevertheless standing, to the great astonishment of all such as hath seen the same.' The Earl of Sutherland began to carry out repairs after that, and the eastern part of the ruin was given a new roof in 1616.

The unfortunate town suffered the depredations of an occupying army again in 1654, this time from a royalist force under the command of General Middleton, Charles II's commander-in-chief in Scotland. Middleton landed at Little Ferry in February and made Dornoch his headquarters. His allies, including the Chief of Mackay, now Lord Reay, joined him there. The small army was beset by internal bickering, and when Cromwell's troops marched north, Middleton withdrew without joining battle. The Mackays, who seem never to have overlooked an opportunity, are reported to have indulged in pillaging before they left: '... the Earle of Sutherland is driven out of his country with his sons, and Middleton hath turned his Lady out of doores, and sent her after him, and his land and estate is exceedingly wasted.'

A proper restoration of the cathedral had to wait until last century. Between 1835 and 1837, the ruined nave was cleared and rebuilt, and the tower, steeple and interior were restored. This work was financed by the Countess of Sutherland and carried out under the supervision of William Burn, the Edinburgh architect who had already renovated St Giles's Cathedral, covering its medieval stonework in the process. The stones of the old nave of Dornoch were ruthlessly employed in the new construction, and much of the thirteenth-century stonework was demolished. The paint and plasterwork added at this time were later removed in 1924, when further restoration tried to undo some of the excesses of Burn's vandalism.

The present cathedral is a simple, impressive building, filled with a pale, golden light reflected from the warm stonework. There are some fine stained-glass windows, and a lightness and airiness under the high vaulted roof that contribute to the sense of peace in the place. There is humour, too, in the gargoyles – mythical beasts and grotesques – around the external eaves. In the churchyard lies the Plaiden Ell, a flat slab with two metal spikes that was used as standard measure for cloth at bygone fairs and markets. Sixteen earls of Sutherland are said to lie buried in the cathedral, and the burial vault of the Duke of Sutherland is behind the altar in the chancel.

Across the square from the cathedral, a line of old and fairly modern buildings makes a pleasing façade. From east to west, they comprise the old jail, now a craft shop and restaurant, the present sheriff court and the old castle. The jail was built in 1844; before that, prisoners had been incarcerated in the old tollbooth and later in the castle. The minister recorded in 1833 that the latter had twenty inmates: three debtors, six smugglers (that is, moonshiners), one thief and ten prisoners sentenced for assaults 'of various kinds'. You can still visit the cells of the Victorian prison and pass through their narrow, black doors. The castle was built as a residence for the bishops in the sixteenth century; it is now an hotel, but the narrow, spiral staircase is still redolent of the building's original purpose. The castle suffered grievously in the various wars and alarums of Dornoch's history until it was eventually restored and made fully habitable last century.

Dornoch became a royal burgh in 1628, and in 1633 the seat of the sheriff of the county. 'The sheriff-shipp-regallitie of Southerland, and enlarging the bounds of the shriff-shipp of Southerland,' reads a contemporary notice, uncertain of its spelling but not of its importance, 'the dismembring the lands of Strath Navern, Edrachillis, Durines, Strath Halledeil, Assint and Terren Koskary from the Shriffdom of Inverness; reserving, nevertheless, to the Erle of Southerland the privilege of pit and gallows, alwais within his own proper lands, either in tenant or tenantdree.' Note the almost absolute powers given to the earl, who was also, in fact, the first sheriff.

Moving away from the centre of the town to the south-east, we come into the Littletown district of Dornoch. Here, in a garden at the end of the short streets, is a low, dark stone inscribed with the date 1722. It marks where an old, demented woman called Janet Horn was tarred, feathered and burnt to death – the last person to be executed for witchcraft in Scotland. She was found guilty of having turned her daughter into a pony and having had her shod by the Devil. It seems highly unfair that Dornoch should bear this dubious honour, for compared to the rest of the country very few witches were brought to trial in Sutherland – only three, apart from Janet, and they were acquitted. Witchcraft became a criminal offence in Scotland in 1563, and the number of trials ran into the thousands before the laws were repealed in 1736. It is impossible for us today to share the cast of mind that enabled so many sections of society to believe in witchcraft. Caithness saw thirty-four accusations and trials, though the outcomes are in most cases unknown. The repealing of the witchcraft laws did not, however, bring an end to the matter. In 1738, when a certain Donald Mackay from Dunrobin was hanged for murdering an old woman, his defence was that he had killed a hare, unaware that the woman, a witch, had turned herself into the animal that had run across his path.

By 1791 Dornoch had five hundred inhabitants, including one schoolmaster, four shopkeepers, one smith, one mason, three house carpenters, the minister, the Sheriff-depute and his clerk. There was no doctor or apothecary.

In 1834 the minister noted improvements in the town: 'Instead of their feal-houses [feal means turf], in which it was scarcely possible to maintain cleanliness, they have now generally neat cottages, built of stone and clay, and harled with lime, having chimnies instead of the fireplace being in the middle of the house as formerly.' For entertainment there was an 'excellent' inn, which also served the mail coach, and two whisky houses. Such a description sums up the changes that were taking place at the time throughout all the villages and towns in the north.

Among the pleasanter aspects of its history, Dornoch can also boast of a golf course dating back to the early seventeenth century. The club gained its title of the Royal Dornoch from Edward VII, and in 1912 Asquith was interrupted during a round by a suffragette. The town also once had a railway station, the site of which is now a small industrial estate where, amongst other things, Highland armour and boomerangs are manufactured.

Plans are now on paper to build a new bridge across the Dornoch Firth. Construction may begin in 1986, and once this bridge is opened, Dornoch may regain some of the prominence it once enjoyed.

The sandy coast of the peninsula is a popular holiday centre. At Embo, three miles north of Dornoch, there is a large caravan park. Embo itself was laid out in about 1820 as a fishing village, and its original features can still be seen in the grid of streets and the cottages built gable-on to the sea. A small pier sticks out among the rocks to the south of the village, but children flying kites are more common than boats there now. The hotel called Grannie's Heilan Hame, once something of a shrine for those who wallow in the nostalgia that surrounds so much of our history, has in its grounds the remains of a neolithic chambered cairn. The venerable stones of the cairn sit rather forlornly, protected by a chain fence from the holidaymakers, a reminder of the first farmers to hack fields from the woodland of the coast.

Further north, where the shore curves around to make the south side of Loch Fleet, are the ruins of Skelbo Castle. The battered, chewed walls surmount a wooded mound overlooking the entrance to the loch and the sea beyond. The castle is first mentioned in a charter granting it to Bishop Gilbert, who later gave it over to his brother Sir Richard, whose tomb we have already seen at Dornoch Cathedral. The first castle was probably built of wood on the motte-and-bailey pattern of the Normans. In the late thirteenth century envoys waited here to greet Margaret of Norway, sole heir to the Scots throne, only to learn of her death *en route* to Scotland. The castle later passed into the ownership of the Sutherland lairds of Duffus. The age of the stonework is very hard to determine, but it is probably fourteenth century.

The hinterland of the Dornoch peninsula is ignored by most travellers, who allow the A9 to bear them past it. A loop of road serves the crofts and farms of the valley of the Evelix up as far as Achormlarie. This district also has a number of sites of archaeological interest, among them the site of another motte-and-bailey castle, at Proncy.

Where the A9 emerges from the woods at Bridgend and begins its descent to the Mound, the traveller is presented with a fine view of Loch Fleet, a repetition on a smaller scale of the view from Struie Hill. On its descent, the road sweeps across the little valley of Cambusavie, passing close to the group of buildings on the hillside that was built in the early 1900s as an isolation hospital for infectious diseases.

The Mound is a long embankment built to carry the main north road across the head of Loch Fleet. When it was constructed in 1816, about forty acres of carse, or marshy land, became available for cultivation. At the north end of the Mound the road swings in a loop around the shell of an abandoned railway station and its overgrown platforms. The eight miles of track from here to Dornoch were opened with much pomp and celebration in June 1902 on a dull, wet day. The line ran across the Mound beside the road – the piers of the old viaduct stick out of the water at the north end – but the tracks were removed after the line closed in 1960.

Loch Fleet is now a nature reserve. The focus of the reserve is about six hundred acres of alderwoods to the west of the Mound.

This area is managed by the Nature Conservancy Council, who have an office at Golspie, and there is a larger reserve run by the Scottish Wildlife Trust along the north shore of the loch. The latter incorporates part of the basin of the Fleet, which at low tide attracts large numbers of seabirds to feed, and pinewoods along the shore, with populations of redstart, crossbill and siskin.

There is another road from Bonar to the Mound. It passes up through Migdale, sweeps by the crofts near the burn called An Uidh, crosses the broad, ill-defined ridge between Sidhean Mor and Meall Mor, hugs the southern shore of Loch Buidhe and runs down Strath Carnaig. There is a standing stone at Dalnamain, and a dun and cairns between here and Little Torboll, where we rejoin the valley of the Fleet before meeting the A9 at the south end of the Mound under the cliffs of Creag an Amalaidh.

Two roads lead up the Achany Glen to Lairg – the A836 on the east and the B864 on the west. Achany Glen is a narrow, steep-sided cleft, densely wooded with birch in places. Through the woods, pylons carry the power lines from Loch Shin. At Shin Falls one can, with luck and in the right season, see salmon leap the tumbling water. The Falls are easily reached along a path from a restaurant and car-park by the B864. They are not high but are noisy and spectacular where the river plunges through a forested gorge. The water is gurly and dark, and splits into cream-coloured foam on the rocks. 'The salmon on the River Shin are very large,' wrote George Rainy in 1790, and he described how baskets placed below the Falls caught the fish as they fell back down the torrent.

Further up on the B864 is the turn-off to Achany House and farm, part of the North of Scotland College of Agriculture. Achany is a typical hill farm in that most of its land is rough hill pasture, and it is used for research into and as a demonstration centre of matters relevant to hill farming. This means primarily sheep; Achany keeps a flock of about eight hundred North Country Cheviots, though it also has about sixty beef cattle.

Above Achany the woods open out and bare moor becomes predominant. Just north of the House, beside the Grudie Burn, a ruckle of stones marks the site of a chambered cairn.

The junction of the A839 and the B864 overlooks a dam across the Shin. A footpath across the spillway affords fine views up to Lairg itself and down the glen.

The centre of Lairg is a triangular open space. It is a busy place with shops, banks and garages, and police and fire stations, and is the main centre for the north-west of the county. From here roads run across the open, undulating plateau of central Sutherland, a windswept region under a vast sky where the clouds roll like ocean tides. From the 'waterfront' at Lairg along the shore of the loch one can see the Shin Dam, with its grey, fortress-like towers. It is the most northerly dam in the country and has three associated power stations – at Cassley, Lairg and Inveran – pumping power into the National Grid.

The North of Scotland Hydro-Electric Board was established in 1943, steered into the statute book by Tom Johnston, Secretary of State for Scotland in the War Cabinet and one of the ablest men ever to have held this crucial office. It was he who ensured that the powers granted to the new Board took account of the social responsibilities of the enterprise. For example, the revenue from power sold to the Central Electricity Generating Board was used to fund the supply of electricity to rural communities in the Highlands and islands. Work began on the Shin Dam in 1954, and the power stations went into action in 1959.

This might be an opportune moment to acknowledge the work of the modern heroes of the Highlands – the linemen. Blizzards and high winds often play havoc with power lines in winter. In January 1984, at one point the engineers had fifty-six separate 'incidents' to deal with, and while the people stoked up their fires and searched out oil lamps, the linemen set off for the hills to find the faults.

From the dam, Loch Shin stretches through the hills for sixteen miles. The parish minister in the 1790s thought that a canal cut from either end of the loch to the sea would 'soon be the means of establishing fisheries, manufactures, commerce and industry, over all the neighbourhood': thus the ideas of the Age of Improvement. Lairg was then, as it is now, a focus for many routes. Gigs began to run weekly to Tongue and Assynt in the 1830s, carrying mail and passengers. The new ease of communication prompted the minister to note 'that the London papers are received at Lairg on the morning of the fifth day from ... publication'.

A feature of the agricultural calendar that fascinates many a visitor to the north is the autumn lamb sale: Lairg has some of the largest one-day sales in Scotland, thirty thousand lambs coming under the auctioneer's hammer in one day in August 1984, for example. The sales are a mixture of carnival and frenzied activity; shepherds and farmers from remote hill farms meet to blether and do business, and their families treat the occasion as a great day out. The lambs are categorized as hill or park, representing their origin and place of upbringing, with the hill lambs fetching slightly lower prices than the usually larger specimens from lowland farms. The sale is the culmination of the shepherd's labour through a fierce winter and spring, in many ways the only showplace for his or her skill. Whose lambs command which prices is the subject of keen interest and comment.

In 1873 the Duke of Sutherland initiated land reclamation between Loch Shin and the River Tirry. Giant ploughs powered by steam traction engines brought eighteen hundred acres of moor into cultivation for hay and turnips. A monument to this endeavour can be found hidden away in forest near the Shinness church. The path to the memorial, a square stone pillar, goes up the east side of the wood and then makes a sharp turn to the west through dark ranks of conifers. 'To Kenneth Murray of Geanies,' reads the inscription, 'to whose devotion to the cause of agriculture and attachment to the Duke of Sutherland and his people these reclaimed lands are the best memorial.' The giant plough is shown in profile. Although the improvers' intentions were of the best, the crofters who were offered parts of the reclaimed land were not impressed: some thought it worthless and blamed 'the inspectors, who had great notions for machinery, but no brains for what was wanted'. Shinness has to this day a pioneering air about it. The rough pasture and patches of heather and rushes are scarred by ditches and stones; Shinness kirk, a claret-coloured wooden building with a corrugated-iron roof, completes the image. Any roadworks or ditch shows what the improvers were up against – the fertile soil is only a thin skin over the reddish, stony glacial clay beneath.

From Lairg the A839 runs down the valley of Strath Fleet. The western part of the strath is desolate, relieved only by the railway line, the road and one or two houses and caravans, but further to the east woods and green fields lend the land a gem-like quality. The road passes through Muie, Ardachu and Tressady to Rogart. Here the strath widens and the Fleet begins to meander along its floodplain.

On the roadside to the south of the river at Dalmore, in July 1968, John Diefenbaker unveiled a monument to Sir John MacDonald, the first Prime Minister of Canada. 'His monument is a nation,' reads the plaque. 'This cairn is but a footnote to his greatness.' Sir John was actually born in Glasgow and emigrated with his family to Canada in 1826, but Dalmore is where his grandfather died, a poor man but in his younger days a wealthy merchant near Skelbo and reputed on his marriage to have thrown a peck of silver into his bride's lap.

Rogart is a neat village, with the hotel, the mart, the post office and the various houses grouped around the railway station. The A839 runs on down the strath to join the A9 at the Mound, but another road struggles up over the hills to the north through a district of scattered crofts to Strath Brora.

4

From Golspie to the Ord

Three miles beyond the Mound the A9 rolls into Golspie. It is a long, strung-out place, the largest town in Sutherland (it deserves to be called a town, rather than a village) and a busy centre, squeezed between the sea and the rounded mass of Beinn a'Bhragaidh. Sutherland District Council has its headquarters here (although the Council meets in Dornoch), the local weekly paper *The Northern Times* is published here, and it also has the only senior secondary school in the county; pupils from the more distant areas stay in hostels and go home only at weekends. It is also an attractive town and has three times won a Britain in Bloom award for being the best-kept village in the north of Scotland.

In 1807 Golspie was described as 'a fishing village ... consisting of only a few thatched huts, partly underground, occupied by fishermen, with three slated houses inhabited by shopkeepers'. The population grew rapidly in the years that followed, as people evicted from the inland straths, particularly Lairg, settled there in the new planned streets. By 1834 the population had reached 450, and the buildings included an inn, a mill, a bank and a manse in a 'neat village of considerable extent'. The inn was described in 1829 as possessing 'every modern convenience' and was run by a Mrs Duncan, a clergyman's daughter. There were alehouses and a school, and a post office whence a gig with room for two passengers ran to Lairg. October saw the annual fair, and there was a lesser fair in May.

The town became the terminus of the northern railway in 1868.

Two years later, a route continuing north to Wick and Thurso was surveyed; it was concluded that the track would have to go inland to avoid the Ord and that, by using a narrow gauge, the cost could be brought down to £4,000 per mile. The Duke of Sutherland was keen on narrow-gauge railways in rural areas and said that if he had known about them earlier he would have adopted their less expensive construction for the Sutherland Railway. The Caithness Railway Company had already been in existence for some time, and that county was alive with rumours and discussion of the 'iron horse'. In 1870 Parliament passed the Duke of Sutherland's Railway Act, allowing the extension of the line to Helmsdale. Work had begun a year before this, and the line, still on the same gauge, was almost complete by the end of 1870. The coming of the railway did not please everyone: the Dornoch Presbytery of the Free Church complained in 1872 of 'more strangers and laxer morals' as a result.

Duchess Millicent, the wife of the fourth Duke of Sutherland, founded a technical college at Golspie in 1903. The college is now part of the High School.

A promontory extends south from Golspie, almost enclosing the basin of Loch Fleet. At its tip is Little Ferry. Trading vessels used to call here, finding a safe anchorage once the sandbars were negotiated, with cargoes of coal, iron and meal. In the nineteenth century a smack operated a monthly service to Aberdeen and Leith. Little Ferry is now a quiet spot with a stone pier and a few small boats, and only decaying wooden pilings to recall its heyday. Some of the older houses nearby must have been merchants' depots, and cut into a bank at the edge of the woods is an ice-house. At the south end of Golspie's Main Street there is a handsome war memorial set in a little formal garden with a representation of the tree of life carved on the reverse side. The nearby public gardens have a barometer set into a stone pillar; this was presented to the local fishermen by the Duke of Sutherland in 1865, another reminder that this was the seat of Sutherland power. From the crest of the old bridge at the north end of the town rises an obelisk with the inscription:

MORFHEAR CHATT
de
Cheann na Droichaite bi
GAIRM

Chlann
CHATTACH
nam Buadh

It it is difficult to translate this resounding Gaelic call to arms but roughly it means: 'The chief of Sutherland from the head of the bridge calls his clan [and remember that 'clan' literally means 'children'] to victory.'

Old St Andrew's kirk has several interesting features, including the Earl of Sutherland's family loft facing the pulpit. Once a chapel, St Andrew's became the parish church early in the seventeenth century. The oldest gravestone in the kirkyard is dated 1659 and bears a Gordon crest and the initials 'HG' and 'IA'.

The dominance of the Sutherland ducal family has its most tangible manifestation in the immense statue of the first Duke on the summit of Beinn a'Bhragaidh. Designed by Sir Francis Chantrey, the figure is thirty feet high and a landmark for miles around. The inscription describes the Duke as 'a judicious, kind and liberal landlord; who identified the improvement of his vast estates with the prosperity of all who cultivated them ... who ... opened wide his hands to the distress of the widow, the sick and the traveller ...', and then, in capitals for emphasis, 'A MOURNING AND GRATEFUL TENANTRY, UNITING WITH THE INHABITANTS OF THE NEIGHBOURHOOD, ERECTED THIS PILLAR AD 1834.' The irony of these words, coming at a time when a goodly proportion of the tenantry were being or had just been evicted to make room for sheep, escaped no one.

The road to the top of Beinn a'Bhragaidh forks on the wooded braes above the Golspie Burn, and the main tarred section continues up Dunrobin Glen eventually to reach Rogart. There are some lovely walks in the woods of Dunrobin Glen; the paths lead to a secluded waterfall.

North of the Golspie Burn, the A9 passes the gates of Dunrobin Castle. The drive is guarded by two square towers; opposite these, through another gateway, are the railway line and the castle's private station, and beyond a statue, of fairly modest proportions this time, of the second Duke, who died in 1861. The main drive leads down to a gravelled yard at Dunrobin. The name means 'fort of Robin', and the first keep was probably built by the sixth Earl, who died in 1427; part of the old structure is still visible to visitors who tour the castle and is easily recognized by its reddish, coarse stonework.

The Sutherland chiefs were descended from Norman knights who were granted lands in Scotland in the twelfth century. Many of the great Highland families – the Sinclairs of Caithness, the Frasers of Beauly and the Grants of Moray among them – sprang from the same source, and their acquisition of property was part of a deliberate policy of the Scots kings who wished to consolidate their hold on the realm by the planting of feudal vassals on whom they could rely. We can trace the Sutherland ancestry to a man called Freskyn who died in about 1170 and who held land in lowland Scotland. One of Freskyn's grandsons, Hugo by name, may have been granted estates in Sutherland by William the Lion, perhaps as a reward for assisting the King in his conquest of Caithness in 1196. In about 1211 Hugo granted land in eastern Sutherland to Gilbert de Moravia, perhaps his cousin. Hugo's youngest son, Andrew, became Bishop of Moray, and his eldest son, William, was made the first Earl of Sutherland by Alexander II in about 1235.

Robin, or Robert, the sixth Earl, came to power shortly after 1370. The stone keep which he raised in a strong position on the raised beaches along the Golspie shore probably replaced an earlier wooden fortress. In 1389 Robin married Margaret, one of the daughters of Alexander, Earl of Buchan, who, besides being a brother of the King, was one of the most powerful men in the north and bore the grim byname 'Wolf of Badenoch'. In an attempt to reconcile the differences between himself and the clan Mackay, Robin met the Chief of Mackay and his son at Dingwall in 1395. But one night, in an incident hauntingly reminiscent of Shakespeare's Macbeth (though not the historical one), Robin's son, incensed by the haughty behaviour of the Mackay chief, rose and stabbed him and his son. For a long time after that, there was no love lost between the Mackays and the Sutherlands.

In 1494 the Gordon Earl of Huntly succeeded in bringing out a statement that John, the eighth Earl of Sutherland, was mad; Huntly followed this with a similar charge against John's son. It was perhaps no coincidence that John's daughter, Elizabeth, who inherited the earldom, was married to Adam Gordon, Huntly's brother. The Gordons were a powerful clan, 'on the make' in the early sixteenth century in Ian Grimble's phrase in his book *Clans and Chiefs*. A struggle arose between Elizabeth and her brother Alexander, who also claimed the earldom. With the might of the Gordons behind her, Elizabeth triumphed, and Alexander's head ended up on a spearshaft at Dunrobin in 1519. Elizabeth ruled for a while, and after her death in 1535 the earls of Sutherland bore the surname of Gordon.

The feud between the Mackays and the Sutherlands continued, although between bouts of fighting and raiding the leading protagonists signed bonds of friendship. Adam Gordon and Iye Mackay signed one at Inverness in 1517; Gordon put his name to another at Abbirsco (Aberscross?) a year later, with John Mackay of Strathnaver. In 1522 Alexander, Elizabeth's son, signed again with John Mackay at Dornoch, on the relics of St Gilbert. On 28 April 1549 the leaders of the three northern clans came together to sign a bond at Girnigoe Castle: George Sinclair, the Earl of Caithness, William, the Earl of Sutherland, and Donald, Chief of Mackay – Mackay could not write and the Bishop of Caithness witnessed his mark.

At the beginning of the seventeenth century the earldom was raised to a regality, giving the earl well-nigh absolute power in his domain. In such situations, the overall rule of the king was invested in the person of the sheriff, an office that in Sutherland was the hereditary right of the earl.

Despite their increasing power, the family fell on hard times in the mid-seventeenth century, according to the three-volume history *The Sutherland Book*. The Earl sold some of his silver plate in Inverness to meet debts, and complained about his sons, who were living it up in London, and his tenants, who were in arrears with their rent. In 1656 he wrote that he was 'als bair as the birke at Chrismess' and six years later resigned the earldom in favour of his son. In 1710 the sixteenth Earl resumed the surname of Sutherland.

Caithness and Sutherland played only a tentative part in the Jacobite rebellions. In his *History of the Rebellion in the Year 1715*, the Reverend Robert Patten listed among the Scottish chiefs the earls of the two counties and Lord Reay and gave a statement of their allegiance: the Earl of Sutherland '1,000 men' and Lord Reay '500 men' were for the House of Hanover, but the Earl of Caithness was described as 'neutral' while most of his '300 men' were against the government. It is significant that, although Caithness was much the more populated county, the Earl could call on so few men; this reveals the difference between a clan society and one where landowners were lairds rather than chiefs. Thirty years later, before the 1745 rebellion, Duncan Forbes noted that the Earl of Caithness 'could raise 1,000 men but many of his followers are now under May, Dunbeath, Ulbster, Freswick, etc, etc' – that is, the various landowning branches of the Sinclair family, who were not bound to each other by clan loyalties.

When the Earl of Mar raised his standard in 1715 to launch a campaign on behalf of the exiled Old Pretender, the Earl of Sutherland rushed home to raise a force against him. With his supporters the Earl devised a plan to take and hold Inverness for the government. Their attack was successful and the town fell to the loyalists three days before Mar himself was defeated at Sheriffmuir near Stirling.

Events in 1745–6 were more dramatic. Sutherland and Lord Reay remained loyal to the government, as did the Earl and Sheriff of Caithness, George Sinclair of Ulbster. The other Sinclairs had Jacobite sympathies but were rebels more in thought than in deed: they toasted Prince Charles's success, and the ladies of the county were reported to have worn miniatures of the handsome Young Pretender around their necks. The Laird of Dunn, in a gesture which was almost a reflection in miniature of the whole rebellion, tried to assemble his tenants to join the Prince's army, but the women hid their menfolk and took over the farmwork themselves. Dunn, overwhelmed by this rejection of his leadership, shot himself.

In early 1746 the rebel army was nearing the end of its retreat from Derby to Inverness. The Earl of Cromarty led an advance force of Jacobites to seize the town and on 18 February drove the defending troops, less than two thousand men commanded by John Campbell, the Earl of Loudon, north to Dornoch. To attack Loudon, the Duke of Perth sent a force across the Dornoch Firth under the cover of fog and led the rest of his men around by Bonar. The two-pronged attack took Loudon completely by surprise: about sixty men and several officers were taken prisoner, Loudon himself retreated to Skye, and part of his regiment went north to Tongue, a happy coincidence for the government as it turned out. Shortly before, Lord Macleod, the son of the Earl of Cromarty, had led a recruiting party to Thurso to try to drum up some support for Prince Charles. Wearing white cockades in their hats, the Jacobites caused great alarm although they behaved with restraint and harmed no one. To escape them, some of the locals went into hiding or fled to Orkney, taking care to bury their money before they left.

In March the rebels marched on Dunrobin to capture the Earl of Sutherland. At Little Ferry they seized four ships with some cannon. Fearing his castle was not cannon-proof, Sutherland fled in an old fishing boat, barely getting out of range of Dunrobin before the rebels arrived. A thick fog obscured the Earl's flight, and they sailed until they put into Cromarty in Ross-shire to get water; later they were picked up by HMS *Shark* and taken to Aberdeen.

One of Sutherland's men, Hugh Monro, escaped from Dunrobin by boat a few days later and wrote to his master to tell what had happened at the castle: 'In less as half-an-houre after your lordship took boat, the rebells, 300 of them, came to Dunrobine ... commanded by M'Donald of Clanronald. They were that night in your lordship's castle and the tennents' houses thereabouts. I had 40 of them under command of two officers. My wife intertained them; but my brother and I went to the hills. Nixt morning the rebells went back to Dornoch, they being alarm'd that Lord Loudon was to attack them.' The Countess of Sutherland had not fled with her husband. Monro reported that 'One of [the rebel] officers had a durk to my Lady Sutherland's brest, to get account where your lordship was, and arms, to which he gote noe satisfactory answer.' The dirk scratched the Countess but she bravely refused to co-operate with information and entertained the officers instead. 'They made a stable of your dining room,' wrote Monro in disgust, and he went on to list the damage. The Jacobites filled the rooms with hay to sleep on, stripped the leather off the chairs, carried off documents, stole the silver plate and a silver candle-snuffer, killed livestock and took horses, and drank all the wine. Meanwhile the men of the Earl's militia had gone into hiding, and the women were smuggling ammunition to them under their hoop petticoats.

By this time the main rebel army was gathering at Inverness. The Earl of Cromarty's men burned mansions at Kintradwell and Crakaig and, to the horror of the people they wanted to recruit, disinterred a corpse at Navidale. Later, two Jacobite officers were murdered in Glen Loth by local men. Cromarty returned to Dunrobin and waited there for his son to return from Caithness; when Macleod came, he had forty-five recruits in tow.

On the day before the battle of Culloden, Cromarty despatched his force, some 350 men all told, south. But the Earl of Sutherland's militia, who had been biding their time in the hills, attacked the rebels at Little Ferry. This small force, about twenty-six men led by an Ensign Mackay, succeeding in dividing the Jacobites and scattering them. Cromarty and his son were captured. Later, in London, they were found guilty of high treason. Cromarty was sentenced to death but was reprieved at the last moment when his wife flung herself at the feet of the King in a plea for mercy.

After Culloden, government troops scoured the country to search out and destroy the last vestiges of rebellion. A troop came after Sinclair, the laird of Scotscalder, who had been too overt in his sympathy for the Jacobites. He fled into hiding, leaving his wife to face his pursuers. She must have been a redoubtable hostess, for she entertained the soldiers so well that after a peremptory search of the house they left happy and slightly unsteady in the saddle.

The present castle of Dunrobin, on its terrace above the sea, has a fairy-tale look. The pointed turrets and towers give it the air of a *château*, a deliberate impression created by Sir Charles Barry in the mid-nineteenth century when he designed additions which were modelled in part on Chenonceaux in the Loire valley. The restoration work was continued and completed by Sir Robert Lorimer in 1921. A large part of the castle is open to the public, and a comprehensive handbook has been published to guide the visitor through the various rooms, hung with paintings and crammed with the furniture, *objets d'art* and paraphernalia of a noble family. Between the castle and the sea, a large formal garden has been laid out in a series of terraces; the geometric designs of the flowerbeds were first laid out in 1850.

The modern phase of the history of the Sutherland family began in 1766, when the seventeenth earl died and was succeeded by his daughter Elizabeth. In 1785 she married the Marquis of Stafford, the scion of an English family that had risen in wealth and power during the Industrial Revolution. Stafford inherited his English estates from his father and a fortune from his uncle the Duke of Bridgewater. By his marriage to the Countess of Sutherland, he added most of that county to his lands and set about implementing ideas of reform and improvement in land-use that led to the eviction and emigration of many of his tenants and which still give rise to heated controversy. Stafford himself was made the first Duke of Sutherland six months before his death in 1833. In this century Dunrobin has had a chequered career: during both World Wars it was used as a hospital, and for a period of several years ending in 1972 as a boys' school.

About a mile and a half north of Dunrobin the A9 passes close to the base of a broch. This broch, at Strathsteven, is accessible to the traveller and shows some of the basic features of its type: the thick double wall with its internal stair and the low entrance passage with a guard chamber and door checks. The broch is a structure characteristic of the centuries surrounding the birth of Christ. The circle of drystone masonry at Strathsteven is the base of a tower that would have risen probably fifty feet above the ground, tapering slightly towards the top. We can only speculate on how any broch was roofed, but it would have been easy to lay timbers and skins across the open ring of stone. Brochs show no evidence of ever having had windows, a fact that leads scholars to think they were built primarily for defence. They are confined in their distribution almost entirely to the north of Scotland, and they are very widespread in the two counties, often standing on hilltops or coastal promontories; the greatest concentration of brochs is found in Caithness, but there are also large numbers in Orkney and Shetland.

The ruins of brochs are commonly referred to as 'Picts' hooses' though they were built before the emergence of the Picts as a readily identifiable culture. It is possible that they were built by the ancestors of the Picts, or even by people whose aim was to keep the Picts out. Whoever they were, the brochs remain as a mysterious, and sometimes awe-inspiring, manifestation of a people's response to their environment; the dry-stone masonry is superb and has not been surpassed by succeeding occupiers of the land. How many of our walls will be standing in two thousand years' time?

The A9 takes us next to the little town of Brora, on a low, slightly windy promontory where the River Brora cuts into the sea. The name is derived from Norse and means 'river of the bridge'; until the Age of Improvement this was the site of the only bridge in Sutherland. The river divides the town into two, almost equal halves, to the north and south of the deep ravine through which it flows, deep, dark and foam-flecked, to the sea. James VI made Inver of Broray, as it was then called, a free burgh of barony in 1601, and the town was the site of the local court until the early nineteenth century. The most curious thing about Brora, however, is that the presence of Jurassic coal seams has made the town a small pocket of industrialization in an otherwise agricultural and moorland landscape.

The first mention of the coal deposits was made in 1529, and the first attempt to open a mine in 1598. Since then the seams have been intermittently exploited. To avoid the risk of explosion underground it is said that the miners once used the phosphorescent heads of dead fish instead of candles to light their labours. The Duke of Sutherland looked to the mine, as to much else, as a means of developing the local economy; he spent £16,000 on sinking a new pit to reach seams 250 feet down, and the works opened in 1812. He also had built a railway track to carry coal from the mine to the new harbour half a mile away. In 1949 the National Coal Board intended to close the mine but the local MP, Sir David Robertson, managed to find an independent operator to keep it open; eventually it did close, in the early 1970s, when it was employing thirty men and producing five thousand tons of coal a year. One day it may open again, as surveys have shown that the reserves of coal are around eight million tons.

Brora grew in size at the beginning of the nineteenth century, its population swollen by tenants evicted from the inland straths. The coal mine was part of the attraction of this stretch of coast, and the minister, writing his contribution for the *New Statistical Account of Scotland* in 1840, described what happened: '... when the tenants were removed from the interior of the county to the coast-side, the poor belonging to this and other parts of the estate, and those who were unable or unwilling to occupy and improve lots of land, settled in the vicinity of the coal-pits, where they were ensured abundance of fuel, without pay or trouble; and living among men in regular receipt of high wages, they were sure to obtain a share of these earnings; but when the works ceased, they enjoyed no such advantages, and, being thrown on their own resources, they soon became a burden on the community.' The population of the town at this time was 280. Of the total area of the parish, the minister estimated that fourteen hundred acres (just over two per cent of the land area) were cultivated, much of it recently 'trenched from the barren waste by the settlers from the hills'; this tilled acreage was shared between a handful of farms and almost four hundred cottar families with an average of two acres each. It is hardly surprising that the community could not support its poor with ease.

There were other industries. Saltpans were opened and a brickworks was founded in 1818. One result of the latter is the terrace of brick houses to the north of the river; the date '1875' is on one gable and the ornate capital 'S' for the ducal family on the other. One industry started in the nineteenth century continues, however, to thrive. The engineering shop erected during the building of the railway in 1872 was converted into a weaving shed and leased by the third Duke of Sutherland to a Yorkshire firm. It fell on hard times and was taken over in 1901 by T.M. Hunter from Wick. He installed plant to carry the manufacturing process from raw wool to finished fabric, making a range of products – tweeds, blankets, rugs and yarns. Business expanded and in the 1920s the mill exported to Europe and North America; about a quarter of the company's products still goes to the United States. The present president of the firm is the widow of the founder's son; it is still very much a family business, though it employs over 150 people. There were spin-offs: in 1913 Hunter set up the Brora Electricity Supply Company, which lit the town for the next twenty-five years. Brora is also the site of Sutherland's only whisky distillery – at Clynelish, just to the north-west of the town. The original distillery was founded by the Duke of Sutherland in 1819 to use the new crops of grain coming from the improved farming in the area. Since then the distillery has gone through several changes of ownership, at present being part of Ainslie & Heilbron Ltd. Clynelish whisky is used in blending and is also marketed as a malt, 'fully flavoured

... fruity and delicious' in the words of one whisky pundit.

Behind the town Strath Brora cuts narrowly through the hills. Most of the lower part of the strath is filled by Loch Brora, at the lower end of which there is a small islet where, it is said, the earls of Sutherland kept a hunting lodge in the Middle Ages. The road through the strath runs by the north shore of the loch to Gordonbush, where the braes draw back a little. Loch Brora is fed by two main streams, the Brora and the Black Water, which unite about one mile west of the loch at Balnacoil. Strath Brora and the road continue west to Dalreavoch, where the river valley parts company with the asphalted way and turns north-westward to form its own, ancient path into the hills.

North of Brora, the countryside undergoes a subtle change. The hills creep closer to the sea, leaving only a confined shelf of raised beach for the road and the railway to follow. Trees become fewer, and there is a keener edge to the salt-smelling easterly breeze. The beach is mile after mile of sand, punctuated by weed-bestrewn clumps of rock where oyster-catchers, cormorants and gulls gather to watch the tides ebb and flow.

Halfway between Brora and Helmsdale the little River Loth tumbles down through the glen of the same name. Before the bridge was built here, travellers had to wade across. The river was described as 'impassable in speats', and a postman was drowned in 1755. When it debouched onto the flat ground around Lothbeg Point, the river used to wind east to enter the sea at Lothmore, but the course was shortened in the late eighteenth century when the Countess of Sutherland had a channel cut directly to the shore south of the Point.

Glen Loth itself offered a convenient route through from the coast to the Strath of Kildonan in ancient times, and an unsurfaced track now threads through the gap, past the ruined broch at Carn Bran and standing stones where the Sletdale glen comes in from the west. Further up on the moors under Beinn Dhorain is the Clach Mhic Mhios. Legend has it that this standing stone was hurled from the summit of Ben Uarie by a one-month-old boy back in the time when the land was inhabited by a race of giants. Another association with Celtic myth is Carn Bran itself, reputed to be the burial place of Ossian's hound Bran.

Coming back to more recent times and to the A9, a stone by the side of the road about half a mile south of Lothbeg marks where the last wolf in Sutherland was killed by a hunter in the early years of the eighteenth century.

The A9 runs on north through Lothmore and Portgower, where it makes a rapid and sudden descent down the face of an old raised beach. Portgower was a small fishing hamlet in the nineteenth century, but there has been no commercial fishing here now for many decades. As the road approaches Helmsdale, it seems to run almost on the beach; in winter, when an easterly gale is blowing, this impression is even more convincing.

A new section of the A9 sweeps the traveller into the centre of Helmsdale. It is a large village, with Golspie and Brora forming a trio of large settlements along the east coast, and it is also a meeting of ways. A broad strath leads north-westward right through the county to the north coast: the whole route is sometimes referred to as Strath Halladale, though properly this name belongs only to the northern section beyond Forsinard; the southern section leading from Helmsdale is better called Strath Ullie, from the Gaelic name for the Helmsdale river – Ullidh, an ancient name that may have pre-Indo-European roots. The name of the village itself is derived from Norse: in the Icelandic sages, it is Hjalmundsdalr, the valley of Hjalmund.

In 1791 the minister of Loth parish lamented the absence of a bridge to cross the Helmsdale. Travellers crossed by foot or on a ferry: Thomas Pennant rode his horse across in 1769 and found the water 'rapid and full of great stones', though that did not stop him from getting down and turning over boulders in a search for lampreys. The old bridge, 'a handsome structure of two arches', was completed in 1811 at the cost of £2,200. Its new neighbour, downstream, which hustles travellers through the village in a flash, was opened in 1972.

Helmsdale had great importance as a fishing centre in the nineteenth century. The first herring-curing station was built by the Sutherland estate in 1814 for a Morayshire firm; an inn and houses were also erected then, and the Duke of Sutherland recruited the engineer John Rennie to design the harbour. Some of the streets in the new planned village were named after the Duke's English estates; hence such non-Sutherland names as Stittenham turn up on the signposts here.

The population of the parish almost doubled between 1801 and 1831, the numbers swollen by emigration from the interior of the county. The completion of the harbour in 1818 boosted the fishing: from a herring 'cure' of about five thousand barrels in 1815, the figure rose in 1839 to 46,571 barrels, half of which were exported. Two hundred boats or more were operating from Helmsdale in the mid-nineteenth century: James Thomson described the curing yards as having 'long been famed as about the most complete on the coast ... fitted up on the most convenient plan, roomy, substantial, and having every necessary appendage in store houses, packing sheds, salt cellars ...'. The harbour was extended in 1839–41 and rebuilt in 1890. When the herring fishing declined at the beginning of this century, white fishing took its place but never reached the scale or grandeur of its predecessor. About 1914 a gale tore the harbour breakwater apart, and further damage in 1921 undermined a lighthouse that stood at the harbour mouth.

The fishing industry here now is but a shadow, a poignant, faint echo of its past. One interesting development, however, is worthy of note: it may be an indicator of the future. In 1959 Alexander Jappy set up a business to collect live crabs and lobsters from the many small harbours around the coast. At a sizeable establishment in Helmsdale, live shellfish were kept in tanks until they were ready to be processed. The firm has also experimented with farming shellfish, hatching and attempting to rear from the larval stages crabs and lobsters; these trials have not been successful, in the sense that they are not commercially viable, but more work along these lines may one day bear fruit. As it is, the northern seas seem to be free from any risk of overfishing of shellfish: there is time.

In 1870 Helmsdale stood at the end of the north railway line. In the following year the Caithness Railway Company and the Duke of Sutherland's company amalgamated and work began on the '59 miles, 1 furlong and $2\frac{3}{4}$ chains' of track to be laid between Helmsdale and Wick. The line was to be known as the Sutherland and Caithness Railway. The Board met for the first time at Dunrobin Castle on 19 September 1871: William Baxter of Brora was appointed engineer in charge of the construction of the Sutherland section. Murdoch Paterson, an engineer from Inverness, had already marked out the route the line would follow from the county march to Wick and Thurso.

The building of the railway was a difficult and lengthy business. There were miles of bog and moor to be crossed, tons of earth and rock to be moved, much of it in winter. The navvies lived in wooden huts, out of touch with village or town, without roads to take. Many fell ill with dysentery or chest complaints. In the winter of 1873–4 they were snowed in, a foretaste of what would happen to many a passenger and train-driver, and they complained of the lack of ministers to attend to their spiritual needs.

Work began at Helmsdale in November 1871, and at Wick in the following summer. On 27 August 1872 the foundation stone of the bridge over the Thurso River at Todholes was laid, and on 3 September the one of the bridge at Halkirk. A locomotive began to run from Thurso in March 1873, carrying ballast, sleepers and rails. The situation in the Strath of Kildonan was similar. Shooting lodges began going up, as the gentry anticipated the easy access to the hills the new line would provide. The last rails were laid and the last spike was driven home on 7 July 1874. Two days later the Duke drove his own engine and carriage from Dunrobin to Wick, covering the seventy-five miles in $4\frac{1}{2}$ hours. There were numerous stops and much celebration, but the party arrived at Wick to find a virtually deserted station. The railway was officially opened on 28 July: trains left Thurso and Wick simultaneously at 5.10 a.m.; at Georgemas the Thurso passengers transferred to the Wick train in a high state of excitement – and relief, because they had had to wait half an hour for it to arrive – and rumbled south to Inverness, reaching there at 12.15 p.m.

To the south of Helmsdale, the crofting districts of Gartymore and West Helmsdale spread along the hillside, the fields running in multi-coloured strips down from the houses. The road that serves this area affords good views of the surrounding coast, and at its highest point, hard by the bridge over a little burn, a stone pillar has a plaque that reads: 'In Memory of the Highland Heroes of the Land League "They laid the foundations that we might build thereon" Gartymore 1881–1981.' Nearby, as if to remind one of the issue at stake, three abandoned houses are falling in on themselves.

For a fuller story of the Land League, we can turn back in time to 5 August 1914 and in place to a field at Caen up the strath from Helmsdale, the site of a special ceremony on that day. On the way north to attend it, William Hasson, a journalist from

Inverness, met the men of Sutherland heading south on 'khaki trains' to war. The parallel with the situation one hundred years before, when the men of the straths had gone off to fight in the Napoleonic wars, did not escape him: then the land had not been theirs, now something had been achieved.

Some twenty-five years had passed since resentment against eviction had, in Joseph Macleod's words, 'burst forth into a flame'. Macleod was a native of Kildonan: in 1882 he determined to do something about the people's grievances. At that time there was much agitation for land reform in the Highlands. Agriculture was in a depressed state, and crofters, at the bottom of the heap on the poorest land, were suffering the worst. Rent strikes took place, and a barrage of letter- and pamphlet-writing spearheaded the backlash to near a century of oppressive landlordism. There was much talk of extending the Irish Land Bill, then making a slow progress through Parliament, to cover crofters. Tenants at Clyth resolved to petition for a government enquiry into their condition, their rents having been raised by over fifty per cent in less than twenty years; 'rack-renting' was the current buzzword. Even the Dean of Guild of Inverness Town Council proposed a motion to petition Parliament for land reform, though the move was defeated. The Duke of Sutherland was attacked in a letter from a Glasgow man called R. Macleod for intending to withdraw the grazing rights of small tenants near Helmsdale. Macleod threw in what was a taunt to arms: 'The deer, the eagle, the catamountain abound in primitive wilderness, but up till now the men have been as tame as sheep under the iron rule of the Gowers [the Duke's family name].'

With three others, Joseph Macleod invited Angus Sutherland to come north to address a public meeting. Sutherland was a teacher at Glasgow Academy and a member of the Glasgow Sutherlandshire Association, and he had been an active agitator on behalf of the Skye crofters whose struggle for land was in many ways the epicentre of the agitation. The outcome of the teacher's visit was the formation of the Sutherland Crofters' Association, which was later to amalgamate with the Highland Land Law Reform Association (HLLRA).

Violence broke out in Skye in 1882. The police battled crofters, many of whom were arrested and brought to Inverness for trial. Evictions were threatened in Kildonan. Meetings in support of land reform were held in the Scottish cities, where exiles' associations kept a close watch on events back home in the north. Simultaneously the landowners and 'big' farmers held their meetings; at one, a speaker condemned the agitators 'who were poisoning the minds of the poor' and charged that they 'should be sunk in a bog'.

The HLLRA was formed in 1882 (later it was to shorten its name to the form in which it is commonly remembered – the Land League): the subscription for an honorary member was one guinea, for a crofter one shiling. At last the government responded and set up a Commission of Inquiry under Francis, Baron Napier. Napier and his five colleagues travelled around the Highlands, taking evidence from crofters, ministers and factors; in 1884 their report was published in five hefty volumes. It remains to this day a remarkable historical document.

Coincidentally with the agitation, the third Reform Act vastly increased the electorate in the Highlands: in Sutherland the numbers entitled to vote rose by over eight hundred per cent, many of them crofters. There were at the time three constituencies covering what is now the one – Caithness and Sutherland, and each was characterized by a small electorate consistently returning unopposed landowner MPs. In the General Election of December 1884, new crofters' candidates stood and land reform became the only issue of consequence. The sitting member for Sutherland, the eldest son of the Duke, who had held the constituency since 1874 but had never been known to say a single word in the House of Commons, suddenly spoke up for land reform; in fact, the change in this noble son's thinking went so far as to recommend the abolition of the House of Lords and the nationalization of land. Angus Sutherland stood against him in 1884, but lost. However, in the next election, in 1886, the Duke's son resigned (though not before trying to introduce his own crofters' bill) and Sutherland won the seat. The two other northern constituencies had already been won by crofters' candidates. The crofter MPs, as they were called, now numbered six, and one of them, Charles Fraser-Mackintosh of Inverness, introduced the Crofters' Bill which received the royal assent in 1886. This did not bring the agitation to an end, neither did it solve many of the problems, but it was the first step.

Joseph Macleod of Kildonan was one of the polemicists of this revolution, now oddly half-forgotten or at least less well remembered than the Clearances. (Iain Fraser Grigor's *Mightier than a Lord* and James Hunter's *The Making of the Crofting Community* are two of the few books devoted to it, in contrast to the many volumes on the Jacobites and the evictions.) 'There is nothing in the world,' Macleod had written, 'so wicked as that lordship in land, which in this country sets both God and man aside in the interests of a few.... The mansions built for the tenants of the wide sheep walks are now tenantless; the crofts are exhausted from want of the rest enjoined; and the sheep walks are choked up with damp and weeds, from excess of rest and want of "the tillage of the poor".' Macleod's arguments were rooted in the teaching of the Bible, as were those of his contemporaries and colleagues, men such as Donald Bannerman of Helmsdale and Hugh Campbell the blacksmith of Reay. On that day at Caen in August 1914, as the nations of Europe were preparing to hurl themselves at each others' throats, the celebrations of the land reform movement began with the singing of Old Hundredth:

> Know that the Lord is God indeed;
> Without our aid he did us make;
> We are his flock, he doth us feed,
> And for his sheep he doth us take.

In the sixteenth century, the earls of Sutherland kept a hunting lodge at the mouth of the Helmsdale river. The first building was put up in 1488 by Margaret Baillie, the widow of the eleventh earl, but it was later demolished and rebuilt in 1615 by Alexander Gordon, the son of the sixteenth Earl. The lodge, or castle, used to stand at the south tip of the river mouth; its last remains were swept away when the new road bridge was built.

It was here, on a July evening in 1567, that one of the earls and his wife sat down to a fateful supper. The Earl sensed that something was wrong with the wine he was drinking and told his son, Alexander, who was late in arriving after making full use of the long day to hunt in Kildonan, not to drink any. But the son of another guest, Isobel Sinclair from Dunbeath, was too thirsty after his day on the hill, and he swallowed a draught of the liquor: he died two days later. The Earl and his wife died after eight days. Isobel Sinclair was arrested on a charge of having poisoned her hosts. She was found guilty but she died, perhaps by her own hand, on the morning before her execution was due. Her motive in committing the murder was explained by the fact that, if the son of the Earl were to die, her own son would be in a position to succeed to the earldom. That the first victim of her plot was the son she hoped to advance seems perfectly poetic. However, many thought that the mastermind behind the murder was really George Sinclair, the Earl of Caithness, a suspicion confirmed for those who believed it when Sinclair took the Earl's son into his guardianship. This was the son whom the Murrays of Dornoch persuaded to flee from Dunrobin, an event that in its turn brought Sinclair and the Mackays marching to sack Dornoch, as described previously.

The A9 climbs out of Helmsdale and rounds the side of Creag Bun-Illidh to Navidale. Ever with an eye for a good place, missionary-priests led by St Ninian settled here early in the fifth century; the name of Navidale is derived from *naomh*, Gaelic for saint, and *dalr*, Norse for a dale or valley. The present churchyard overlies where Ninian had his chapel, which, according to Sir Robert Gordon, was finally destroyed by a fire in 1556. Navidale is a pleasant, green bowl above the sea – the last cultivated acres before the road twists up to the Ord, the border with Caithness. We shall cross it presently, but first we must return to Helmsdale and explore its strath.

The road through the strath is the A897, running along the north-east side of the river as it rushes and winds through its floodplain. The strath is pockmarked with signs of ancient settlement. Archaeologists have uncovered many of them: at Kilphedir there is a good example of a hut settlement, and there are the marks of a neolithic field system along the Caen Burn. The traces of this early settlement and agriculture are not always easy for the untrained eye to spot, but there are maps and books to guide those who wish to seek them out. The carbon dating of charcoal deposits from the floors of the huts show that they were lived in around 2000 BC, and the total number of hut circles in Sutherland must run into thousands.

More obvious and more remarkable remains of the neolithic civilization are to be found in the complexes of standing stones throughout the two counties. A few miles up the road from

Kildonan, on the braes above Learable, there is a collection of standing stones, stone rows and cairns. The stone rows in particular have been interpreted by some scholars as neolithic almanacs, used by their builders to observe and predict astronomical events. An understanding of the march of the seasons is, of course, crucial in an agricultural society, no less to a primitive one than to ourselves. The progress of the sun, moon and stars would tell a neolithic farmer when to prepare his ground, when to sow, when he might expect the salmon to begin their runs up the river, when he should hurry to glean the harvest before frosts and gales could tear the future from his grasp. The stone rows are mute but they hint at the sophisticated response 'primitive' people made to their environment.

The scattered district of Kildonan has a long and honourable history. St Donnan ministered to the Picts here and gave his name to the place. A stone slab with a cross near Kildonan Farm may be a relic of his time. The parish church nearby was built in 1786; the pulpit is said to show the footprints of the Reverend Alexander Sage, who was minister here at the beginning of the nineteenth century and whose two wives are commemorated by a stone in the churchyard.

Like other straths in Sutherland, Kildonan suffered during the Clearances. In 1812 the Sutherland estate divided the district into sheep-farms and made arrangements to resettle the resident population on the coast. However, when a group of factors, shepherds and valuers came to inspect the land around Suisgill, they were met by men armed with clubs who told them that, if sheep were brought there, bloodshed might result. In February 1813 John Bannerman of Kildonan wrote to the Sheriff in what was to him a foreign tongue to explain the people's position:

> ... we never was, neither is but Loyal and Submitive to all the laws and Taxs laid on us by Government ... neither are we seeking any of Lady Stafford's land without paying an equal to any other that may gate it ... we expected that Mr Young [the Duke's factor] would give us the first offer of our present possessions ... a good many of us has our children Serveing in the 93rd and was promised to continue their parents in their possessions during paying regularly the yearly rents....

The last statement refers to the fact that many tenants were given to believe by army recruiting parties that their tenancies were safe while their sons served the Crown. Also, one should note that the tenants could not hope to match the rents that sheep-farmers could afford.

Coming twenty years after the sheep drive at Strath Carron, this resistance from the people of Kildonan evoked a similar fear of revolt. The Countess of Sutherland and her husband were at a loss to understand their tenants' intransigence, especially when they resisted persuasion and renegotiated terms of resettlement. It was as much a clash of cultural values as callous oppression. The army was almost called out to enforce the landowner's rights but, after some weeks, the Kildonan folk accepted the inevitable. Many went to settle in Caithness; many more emigrated to Canada, to the Red River settlement in Manitoba. One of them was called George Bannerman, and his great-grandson, John Diefenbaker, became prime minister of Canada in 1957. On the wall of Kildonan church, Diefenbaker unveiled a plaque in 1968 to mark these events.

On a happier note, Kildonan was the scene in 1868 of a remarkable gold rush. In that year, when Robert Gilchrist came home after seventeen years in the Australian goldfields, something stirred the prospector's instinct in him, and he started panning for the precious metal in the gravel beds along the junction of the Kildonan burn and the Helmsdale river. His success attracted others, and by April 1869 hundreds of men were seeking their fortunes. Their tents and shacks were christened Baille an Òr – 'the town of gold'. J. Peacock, the Duke of Sutherland's factor, visited it, bringing gifts of bread, beef and beer for the diggers, and initiated a riotous celebration: 'Nearly 300 ... partook of Your Grace's bounty,' wrote Peacock to the Duke, who was residing in quieter surroundings at Trentham at the time. The church at Kildonan was cleaned out and restored for the prospectors' use, and Mr Adams, a Brora photographer, came up with his camera to record the scene.

In that frantic summer, £12,000 worth of gold was won. Then, tired of the diggers' wild behaviour, the Duke withdrew their permits. The gold rush was over. Later attempts to exploit the deposits were made in 1895 and 1911, but the diggings were 'sadly found wanting'. Today Baille an Òr is a flat expanse of heather, bracken and grass on the north-east side of the Kildonan road, where it loops across the burn. Stones scattered in the vegetation are clues to where the shacks stood. There is still gold to be found here: a few hopefuls pan along the burn, more for fun than in anticipation of wealth.

To the north of Kildonan the strath opens out. A large stream, Abhainn na Frithe, runs in from the west by Loch Badanloch, and the Bannock Burn accompanies the main road and the railway line northwards.

Kinbrace is a small, peaceful place. The village clusters around the station and the junction of the B871 and the A897, at the centre of a wide landscape of moor and field. It was not always so tranquil here: this was a crossroads for the cattle-raiders of the Middle Ages, and earlier still it marked an uneasy boundary between Celtic and Norse peoples. To the north-west of Kinbrace rise the prominent peaks of the Griams. Ben Griam More falls short of two thousand feet but it looks higher, rising from the moorland, and there are substantial crags on it and its smaller neighbour Ben Griam Beag. To the west of Ben Griam More is another conspicuous hill, called Beinn a'Mhadaidh – 'the mountain of the wolf'. The valley between it and some hills to the west is called in the Statistical Account of the parish, published in the 1790s, Bealach nan Creach, 'the pass of the plunder', and probably marks a route taken by the caterans driving stolen livestock.

Kinbrace was also the most probable site for the centre of power of an important Celtic-Norse family whose exploits are described in the *Orkneyinga Saga*. The progenitor of this clan was called Moddan; one of his daughters, Helga, became the mistress of Hakon Paulsson, Earl of Orkney, and another daughter, Frakokk, connived in many of the plots and dynastic struggles that tore at the fabric of the Norse earldom throughout the twelfth century. One of Frakokk's grandsons, Thorbjorn Clerk, killed Rognvald Kali Kolsson, the founder of St Magnus Cathedral in Kirkwall, in 1158. Frakokk herself came to a fiery end at the hands of Svein Asleifarson, after some of her followers had burned Svein's father to death in his house. In the words of the Saga: '... Svein and his men went to the farmstead and looted everything they could lay their hands on, then set fire to the house and burned everyone inside to death. That is how Frakokk died.'

On the summit of Ben Griam Beag are the remains of the

highest hill fort in Scotland: a stone wall, six feet thick, encloses a space of about one hundred thousand square feet, a refuge to which the Iron Age inhabitants of the valley may have fled for shelter during times of war, and a commanding seat of power for a local chieftain.

The district around Kildonan and Kinbrace is traditionally the home territory of the clan Gunn, at least since the fifteenth century, whither they were driven by more powerful families in Caithness. We shall return to the earlier history of the Gunns later. In the strath, their centre of power was at Kilearnan, about two miles south of Kildonan on the south bank of the Helmsdale. From here they played their part in the plots and counterplots between the various clans, shifting their allegiance from Sinclair to Sutherland according to how they thought their best interest lay. The house at Kilearnan was burnt down in 1690 in an accidental fire during the preparation of gunpowder for a hunting expedition. Later, the chief's family moved to Badanloch.

5

From the Ord to Wick

Just beyond the Navidale Hotel one can see a green track winding down by the clifftop. This is the start of the old road across the Ord, a route notorious among travellers for its steepness, bad weather and its precarious position above the sea. Pennant found the cliffs higher and more horrible than Penmaen Mawr in Wales and wrote that the moors gave the place 'a black and melancholy look', a view modern travellers may find easy to endorse. Bishop Robert Forbes, in 1762, was not so easily put out: 'Its Steepness, and being all along on the very Brink of a Precipice, are the only Difficulties,' he wrote, 'for otherwise it is one of the finest Roads in the World, being so broad that in most places two Coaches might pass one another....' It was to be several decades before coaches did make it over the Ord and, despite his nonchalant prose, even Forbes walked beside his horse. The first proper road was not built until 1811.

The modern road holds perils too. In winter it is frequently blocked by drifting snow; at these times the police close snowgates at Navidale and Berriedale. Before the introduction of the gates, three motorists lost their lives in a blizzard in 1978. One man, a commercial traveller for ladies' underwear, survived entombment in his car in the snow by wrapping himself in layers of tights. These dangers are, however, exceptional and the crossing of the Ord is seldom the adventure it once was.

From the heights of the Ord one can see the stark coastline of Caithness stretching away into the distance, a wall of rock running almost without a break for thirty miles as far as Wick.

On this high, windy spot it takes little imagination to see in the mind the gibbets that were erected here in the seventeenth century to hang some of the outlaws and broken men who haunted the border in the time of the clan feuds.

Two miles north of the Ord the road sweeps in a curve around the white farmhouse of Ousdale. There was once an inn here, where the mail coach could get a change of horses and where a choice of teas or coffee was available to travellers. The Ousdale Burn runs down through the centre of the valley; where it cuts through a steep-sided gully close to the sea stand the ruins of one of the best-preserved brochs in Caithness.

On the north side of the valley, where the road clambers up once again to the moors, a track leads off to the right, to a monument and the site of the village of Badbea where tenants evicted from the Langwell estate settled for a time. The story of the Langwell evictions illustrates the absolute power that landlords held at the turn of the nineteenth century. There were once several small villages in the area of Ousdale as well as a meal mill, the inn and a whisky distillery. Robert Sutherland, the proprietor of Langwell in the mid-eighteenth century, was an eccentric free-spending character, given to unusual dress and a copious consumption of wine. On one occasion, dining with a small number of guests, he instructed a servant: 'John, slack a dozen corks of wine, then go downstairs and take your dinner, and when you have done, come up and slack another dozen.' In 1775 he was forced to sell his estate for a little over £6,500 to William Gray, who had been Provost Marshal of Jamaica. Twelve years later Gray sold the estate for £8,000 to Lady Janet Sinclair, the wife of Sir John Sinclair of Ulbster. Langwell became the laboratory for many of Sir John's experiments at improvement. Some, such as his release of nightingales to enliven his plantations, failed, but his most significant innovation succeeded in a way that altered the face of the north. He imported five hundred Cheviot sheep.

We shall return again to the life of this indefatigable improver, but it is worthwhile to examine the philosophy that underpinned his ideas. In 1795, in a book called *General View of the Agriculture of the Northern Counties and Islands of Scotland*, he wrote that the proprietor of land '*is properly a Trustee for the public* [his italics], invested with the possession of a certain tract of country, partly for his own, but principally for the general benefit ...'. He listed the duties of a landlord and numbered among them the obligation to treat tenants fairly. Although he admitted that 'some individuals' would have to be removed from their tenancies, and he himself did this, he thought that they should be shifted into small villages: 'Both humanity, and ultimately the interest of the proprietor himself, however, seem to require that a plan of so extensive and so complicated a nature should not be too rashly gone into; and, in particular, that any considerable body of men should not be removed from their ancient places of residence, until not only proper houses and possessions were prepared for their reception, but also until proper means of employing them are secured.' These were ideas not shared by all the improving landlords in the Highlands.

The flock of Cheviots at Langwell throve 'to the astonishment of the shepherds, who were strangers to the country, and of the natives, who thought that sheep were so delicate an animal, that they ought to be housed in the winter season'. By 1795 the number of sheep had increased to about two thousand, and by 1800 to three thousand. Ousdale was let out as a sheep-farm in 1804, and the tenants there were moved to Badbea; twenty-eight families eventually chose to settle there and hacked out plots of cultivation on the steep braeside. The monument was erected in 1911 by the descendants of some of these families and lists the names of the inhabitants of this exposed village. The ruined houses are still plainly visible, with flourishing whins and foxgloves in their hearths. Life at Badbea was hard. It is said that children had to be tethered if left unattended lest they fell over the cliffs. The new road over the Ord bypassed the settlement and, as the years went by, the people drifted away to more hospitable localities.

Sir John Sinclair sold the Langwell estate in 1813 to an Edinburgh lawyer of Caithness descent, James Horne; in 1858 it was sold again by Horne's nephew to the fifth Duke of Portland. With each sale the value of the estate increased considerably, the Duke forking out £90,000 for his purchase.

North of Ousdale, the A9 provides a fine view of the mountains of Caithness. The highest, Morven, is a shapely cone, 2,313 feet high, and a landmark for almost the entire county. To the east the ridge of Scaraben with its three summits rises to 2,054 feet, and around and between these two mountains are a scattering of smaller peaks – Salvaich, Smean, Carn Mor and Maiden Pap. The bare hills are riven by deep, sheltered straths, the first of which, the course of Langwell Water, joins the second, the Berriedale, just before the merged waters rush into the sea. From the top of the south brae of Berriedale, before the long, steep descent to the strath floor, the traveller has a fine view of the valleys, unusual in Caithness in that they are well wooded. On the brow of the promontory between the Langwell and Berriedale straths stands Langwell House, the home of Lady Anne Cavendish-Bentinck, grand-daughter of the sixth Duke of Portland and the present owner of the Langwell estate.

The village of Berriedale fills the bottom of the strath. The new bridge across the river was opened in 1963 and has made this section of the A9 considerably easier for the motorist to negotiate, although the tight hairpin bend on the north brae has still to be taken with care. The old bridges age gracefully, neglected by the travellers flashing past above them, but it is a nice spot to linger for a little while. This part of the village includes the war memorial, the post office and the old smiddy (smithy), whose gable is crowded with rows of antlers. The other half of the village is on the seaward side of the road. The gorge of the burn is narrow here, and its mouth is almost blocked by a crag that forces the stream to dogleg into the sea across a shingle beach. On the top of the crag, a nesting place for gulls, one can see a few courses of masonry, all that remain of the medieval castle of Berriedale.

Up on the braes under Langwell House there are the ruins of another castle – Achastle, whose history has tumbled into obscurity with its walls, though it is known to have been a stronghold of the Dunrobin Sutherlands. The straths of Berriedale and Langwell were settled long before the Middle Ages, however, and there are numerous brochs, chambered cairns, souterrains (underground storage chambers) and other evidence of prehistory along the valleys as far as Morven itself.

The modern estate of Langwell runs to 55,000 acres and includes the districts of Ousdale and Braemore, on the north side of Scaraben, as well as Berriedale. One of the main activities is the harvesting of the deer herds that roam more or less freely on the moors. There are about three thousand head of deer on the estate – mostly red, though there are also fallow, roe and sika – and about 250 are shot every autumn by a team of stalkers. There is some shooting by sportsmen but most of the stags and hinds are culled by the stalkers, highly skilled men who know the habits of deer and are excellent marksmen. The carcases are brought off the hill by tracked vehicles. An average 'harvest' is fourteen metric tonnes of venison. The deer herd is managed to a considerable extent. The opening of the railway line through the Strath of Kildonan created an artificial barrier that deer could not cross, and stags have to be introduced to Langwell to maintain the quality of the breeding stock; before the railways opened, there was sufficient migration among the deer to make this unnecessary. In the winter the deer's diet is supplemented with hay, minerals, urea and salt; and this is the time of year when the traveller is most likely to see the herds close to the road.

Langwell estate employs about twenty-five people on a full-time basis. Other activities include the farming of a ewe flock numbering seventeen hundred and a sixty-strong beef-cattle herd, forestry, horticulture (the estate gardens are open to the public on certain days, and a garden centre offers plants for sale) and, a new venture, the bottling of spring water for the luxury table-water market.

On a lonely braeside several miles up the valley of the Berriedale Water there is a memorial to the Duke of Kent who was killed here on the night of 25 August 1942 when his plane, a Sunderland flying boat, crashed into the moor in thick fog.

The Berriedale braes and the Ord make it clear why Caithness remained for so long isolated from the rest of Scotland. Beyond Berriedale the bare, undulating plateau that makes up most of the county stretches interminably northward under an infinity of sky. This is a place different from the Highlands. Neil Gunn described Sutherland as alluring and feminine, and Caithness as elemental and masculine; on the other hand, H.V. Morton thought Caithness 'a strong, blonde Viking maiden at her spinning wheel'. Make of that what you will, but the difference between the two counties that becomes apparent beyond Berriedale is real, tangible and of ancient vintage.

Like Berriedale, Dunbeath crouches at the mouth of a sheltered strath. From the A9 on its southward approach to the village, one can see the strath extending to the west, a fold in the hills filled with birch, the river running past the foot of the steep brae, and the little harbour at its mouth. Dunbeath means 'the fort of the birch trees', and in prehistoric times it was the nucleus of a settlement. Opposite the post office, a minor road leads off to the small township of Braemore, in a secluded dale on the upper reaches of the Berriedale Water.

The A9 drops into Dunbeath down a short, steep brae, connecting a hairpin bend at the top and a sharp turn at the bottom across the old bridge. The latter, built by Telford in about 1812, copes as best as it can with heavy modern traffic. Much concern has been voiced in recent years about it and the brae, the most extreme opinion being that the A9 is in imminent danger of sliding into the river below, an event that would cut Caithness off more effectively than any winter blizzard. It is not likely to be long, however, until a new bridge is built to allow its predecessor a well-earned retirement.

The harbour at Dunbeath dates from the beginning of the nineteenth century, when it was developed to take part in the herring boom of those years. In 1838 seventy-six boats were fishing from here; some of the old buildings from this busy time can still be seen, and there is a fine example of an ice-house set into the brae on the north side of the harbour basin. The river runs down through the harbour, debouching through a shingly bed between the old quay and a modern breakwater constructed from concrete dolos. A path from the village crosses the river and takes one along the shore under the grassy cliffs to Dunbeath Castle, a distance of about half a mile. The castle can be glimpsed from the A9 south of Dunbeath but the best view is obtained from this path, which passes through Balcladich, 'the township of the shore', its name another reminder of the area's past, and by some caves where seals were hunted two centuries ago.

The castle occupies a prominent position on a crag above the sea. It is harled and painted white, and still occupied. Most of the present structure dates from the seventeenth century and was built under the direction of John Sinclair, a son of the Sinclair lairds of Mey, who bought it in 1624. The castle does, however, go back further than that, perhaps to the fourteenth century, but the story of its youth has been largely lost.

Perhaps the most dramatic moment in its history occurred in April 1650, when it was besieged and captured by the troops of the Marquis of Montrose. We first met the Marquis at the scene of his final defeat at Carbisdale; now it is time to describe the events that led up to that encounter. In March, Montrose arrived in Orkney from the Continent to start his bid to raise the country in support of the exiled Charles II. He crossed the Pentland Firth with seventeen hundred men, mostly Danish and German mercenaries but including some Orkney levies, and marched to Thurso, where he raised the royal standard and issued a proclamation summoning all true subjects of the King to come forward in arms. A few did, but Lord Reay and the Earl of Caithness remained cannily at home. Montrose may have sensed from this reluctance among his peers that his mission was difficult, if not doomed. Before he left Orkney, he had written to the King: '... I can make yr Mas no other humble acknowl-edgement, bot with the more alacrity and bensell [force] abandon still my lyfe to search my death for the intrests of yr Mas honor and seruice....' He led his troops south and laid siege to Dunbeath when he could as easily have passed it; it has been suggested that he took the castle so as not to have an enemy stronghold at his back. The siege lasted two days, the Sinclair inmates of Dunbeath surrendering when their water supply ran out. Montrose left a detachment to occupy the castle but they surrendered when they received the grim news from Carbisdale that their leader had been defeated.

Dunbeath was the birthplace in 1891 of Neil M. Gunn, and the river, the village and the strath are the inspiration behind many many of his novels, including his major works *The Silver Darlings, Highland River* and *Sun Circle*. In common with many of his generation and others before and since, Gunn left Dunbeath to pursue a career in the south, in his case as a civil servant, but it is clear from his prose that Dunbeath never left him. Gunn achieved an international reputation as a novelist before his death in 1973, and he is the foremost writer to have come from the two counties. A considerable number of writers have, however, drawn on their lives in Caithness and Sutherland; among contemporary authors, one can name David Morrison, Arthur Ball, George Gunn and Donald Campbell, all of whom have expressed something of the spirit of the place in poetry, prose and plays.

To the north of Dunbeath the A9 passes close by the Laidhay Croft Museum. The neat, long, whitewashed croft was opened as a museum in 1974 after four years of restoration work. The building is typical of the small farms that were the main kind of settlement in the area in the nineteenth century: the byre, living-quarters and stable are in one continuous line under the same roof and are built from local whinstone rubble bonded with mud mortar. The adjacent barn shows an example of a cruck roof, where the crucks, the ancestors of rafters, extend to the ground to support the weight of thatch above. To step into the crofthouse is to step back in time – even the smell, a mixture of dust, peat and whitewash, is authentic. The exhibits, which are arranged in as natural a fashion as possible, were donated to the Laidhay Preservation Trust by local people in such abundance that it took four people working full time for three months to catalogue them, and they include a collection of harness and old agricultural implements. In 1978 Laidhay won a Museum of the Year award.

The A9 continues on through Janetstown, beside the last and the smallest of the straths in south-east Caithness. The village is more commonly known as Latheronwheel, an obscure name whose origins are almost impossible to unravel. The first element, 'Latheron', is interpreted in *The Caithness Book*, edited by Donald Omand, as being from the Gaelic *lathair roin* – 'the place of seals'. George Watson, in a brief but fascinating pamphlet *Caithness Place-Names*, published in 1982, derives it from either *ladhran*, Gaelic for prongs or claws, or *hlatha*, Norse for a barn or a pile of stones. The second element in the name may be the Gaelic *fadhail*, a ford, as Watson thinks, or *tuil*, a flood. The name is pronounced 'letheron' locally, and this has given rise to the attractive derivation that, in the old coaching days, drivers were advised when approaching the braes to apply 'leather on wheel'. Janetstown itself is named after the mother of Colin Dunbar, who laid out the village in 1853.

The small harbour at Janetstown is used by only a handful of local boats. A rock stack rises prominently on the south side, and an old bridge with a single span shows where the old coast road crossed the Latheron Burn. A nearby piece of wall is the only remaining fragment of Latheron Castle, which was probably built by the Sinclairs around 1635 but which was already derelict a century later.

The Long Cairn at Camster: the entrance to one inner chamber can be seen on the left and, in the foreground, a horn of masonry enclosing the 'arena' at the end of the cairn.

The square keep and the chimney head of Castles Girnigoe and Sinclair, built on a rock spur near Noss Head.

The Castle of Mey, the Queen Mother's residence in Caithness.

Undersea pipelines destined for the North Sea being manufactured near Keiss.

The most northerly point of the British mainland –
Dunnet Head.

The parish church at Dunnet dates in part from before the
Reformation.

The versatility of flag-stone – an old cheese press on a Caithness farm.

Old St Peter's Church, Thurso.

The foundations of the houses of Rossal in Strathnaver.

The outer chamber of Smoo Cave.

The old church at Balnakeil.

Looking east from the lighthouse at Cape Wrath.

Part of the large fishing fleet at Kinlochbervie.

Scourie Bay, with Handa Island visible offshore.

Crofts at Oldshore, near Kinlochbervie.

About one mile north of Latheronwheel is Latheron itself. Here the A895 leaves the A9 and strikes out across the moors of central Caithness towards Thurso. Known as the Causewaymire, this road was built under the direction of Sir John Sinclair at the end of the eighteenth century. It runs through a countryside that is empty of human habitation except for a few farms, though there are several abandoned houses that show that these inland moors were once more intensively farmed. The road affords the traveller wide, free views of an ocean of heather and grass extending without interruption to the grey, hazy peaks of Morven and Scaraben. What you think of it will probably depend on the weather when you see it, for the light in the northern sky is as much an element in the scenery as the vegetation and the rocks. In spring, when the first flush of growth is hesitantly greening the moors, the light seems to come from within the earth itself; in summer, shifting patterns of cloud spread swathes of colour and shade over the ground; the winter sun brings an infinite range of subtle greys into play, and you can watch the curtains of sleet pass far away across the hills.

Six miles up the Causewaymire from Latheron is Achavanich. A minor road leads from here back to the coast at Lybster, passing on the way through the Rumster Forest where the conifers are upstaged by the 760-foot television mast of the Independent Broadcasting Authority and several other communications towers, including one that is part of the United States Navy early-warning system. A more ancient structure lies in a grassy field at the south end of Loch Stemster not far from Achavanich: almost forty stones are arranged in the shape of an elongated horseshoe opening to the south. Again, we can only guess at what made our neolithic ancestors erect such a structure, but it probably combined religion with astronomy and agriculture.

The remains of a broch scar a little mound on the east shore of Loch Rangag by the A9. This broch has the name of Greysteel's Castle after a ne'er-do-well who made it his home and the base for his marauding excursions on passing travellers. Greysteel was reputed to have discovered the secret of making whisky from heather, and was murdered by two men from Watten when he refused to divulge the magical process.

Caithness and Sutherland are rich in folklore; there are far too many tales of witches, fairies, mermaids, smugglers and weird doings to include in a single book. George Sutherland, the minister of Bruan, collected and published a selection of tales in 1937 in his *Folk-Lore Gleanings and Character Sketches*, from which comes this story about a witch called Fitheach who lived in the Latheron-Forse area.

Fitheach's home was a turf hut, filled with strange objects – curious stones, hair ropes, ravens' feathers (her name means 'raven'), cows' hair – that immediately marked her down to her neighbours as a witch. She was feared but tolerated in the community; it did not do to offend a person who had mystical powers. Fitheach became very friendly with a particular family, and it was noticed soon afterwards that, while the cattle in the district began to give less milk than usual, the number of cheeses drying outside the home of this family continued to increase. Fitheach was suspected but no firm evidence of her guilt could be established. Then it was observed that a hare was frequenting the cattle pasture, a hare that no dog could catch, a hare that a dog belonging to the family with the cheeses would not even chase, a hare that when disturbed always fled in the direction of Fitheach's hut. One bold fellow set a snare, pegging it into the ground with a piece of rowan, a tree capable of countering witchcraft. The snare caught its prey but, instead of a hare, it was Fitheach in the noose. She gave the man back his snare and told him never to set it again in her path. Bad luck came on the man, and he drowned in the Thurso river a few months later.

North of Latheron, the A9 passes Latheron church, which overlooks the sea and is a good place to stop at to take in the southward sweep of the coast. The old graveyard is extensive and crowded, and on a brae high above the church, on the other side of the A9, is a belltower, placed where it was thought the bell could be heard over a wide area. The Clan Gunn Society are working to convert the church into a museum, which should be ready to open its doors in 1985.

Continuing northward we come to Forse. The road crosses the Forse Burn by a mill, and shortly beyond a farm road leads down to the sea, to a cliff-bound promontory and the ruins of Forse Castle. There is little left of the keep and the triangular courtyard and outbuildings of this eyrie, but the masonry and the construction mark it as being probably of Norse origin, of a similar age to the castle of Oldwick. In later times it was the seat of a branch of the Sutherland family. The castle was left to crumble into decay in the eighteenth century when the owner moved to more comfortable surroundings further inland at Forse House, now an hotel.

The largest village between the Ord and Wick is Lybster. The A9 passes through the north end of the village, whence the houses run towards the sea along a mile-long street. At the south end a road drops sharply to the fine harbour, fitting snugly into the bay where the Reisgill Burn plunges dramatically through a gorge. In the parish church lies a stone incised with a cross that was found on the brae above the harbour. The old name for Lybster bay – Haligoe, 'the holy geo' – and the discovery of a graveyard during the building of the harbour indicate strongly that this little bay was an ecclesiastical centre at one time.

As a village, Lybster owes its existence to Patrick Sinclair, the local laird and a cousin of Sir John Sinclair. After a career in the army, Sinclair retired to Caithness in 1784. He extended his home, the Ha' (now Lybster Mains), planted trees, drained land and carried out other improvements, spending money to such an extent that he was arrested in 1804 for bankruptcy. It is a testimonial to his character and his popularity that some of his tenants chased after the arresting officers to secure his release; after his debts were settled, he returned to Lybster to a triumphal welcome.

In 1810 Sinclair built a pier at the mouth of the Reisgill Burn to encourage the herring fishery. The village grew rapidly, the incomers including people evicted from Sutherland, and in 1817 Lybster was recognized as a fishing station by the Fishery Board for Scotland. During the same period, Telford's new road reached the village. After Sinclair died in 1820, his son continued his development plans and laid out the streets around the square at the south end, where the old coast road had passed. Some of the houses here are built in a fine vernacular style and have dates – for example, 1802 and 1833 – above their porches.

By the late 1830s, there were 101 boats at Lybster, making it the third largest herring port in Britain: along the coast from Dunbeath to Clyth, nearly three thousand people were directly involved in the fishery. A traveller in 1829 noted: 'After passing Clythness the bay between that point and the Ord of Caithness lay before us in great beauty, studded all over, as far as the eye could reach, with square-sailed boats, all anxious to secure a portion of the finny spoil, while the nets, stretched to dry upon land, gave the fields a dusky coating of a very unusual appearance.' In the parish, the minister counted twenty-six public houses but thought that six would have been enough. The harbour was rebuilt in 1849 and extended to accommodate the fleet. The lighthouse was added in 1884, but by this time the herring fishery was already in decline.

The traveller will have noticed by this time the distinct Caithness accent with its broad, flat vowels; it is mistaken for Irish by many and is a speech quite different from the Highland lilt encountered in Sutherland. The north-eastern corner of Caithness has never been a Gaelic-speaking area; the Norse settlement in the tenth and eleventh centuries was so complete that their language, having overriden the Pictish speech of an earlier era, persisted as a Norn dialect probably until the fifteenth century, when it was replaced by Scots.

The majority of Caithness place-names are derived from Norse; the ending '-ster', characteristic of Caithness, is a contraction of the Norse *bolstathr* (a farmstead. Another Norse derivative is 'goe', meaning a cleft in a rock face or a cliff; the word is pronounced 'gyeo'). Of course, Gaelic also borrowed words from Norse: *klett*, a rock stack, became *cleit* in Gaelic and 'clett' in Caithness dialect; *skarf*, a cormorant, became *sgarbh* and 'scarf'. Other Caithness words from Norse are 'maa', a seagull, and 'trosk', a fool, from the Norse for codfish, a reference to the gawkish expression on a cod's face. The way words have changed over the centuries makes a fascinating linguistic trail linking history with the present.

To complicate the picture still further, Gaelic was the predominant language in the parishes of Latheron and Reay until quite recently, the tongue of most of the nine per cent of the Caithness population who spoke it in the 1881 census. The boundary between Gaelic and Scots was the burn of East Clyth, four miles north of Lybster, where in 1840 the minister noted: 'On the east side ... scarcely a word of Gaelic was either spoken or understood, and on the west side the English shared the same fate.'

The coastal areas of Caithness from Lybster northwards

towards Wick are rugged and hummocky, moorland sharing the land with fields, and all open to the sky and the wind. The crofts and steadings crouch low across the land, nodes in a network of fences and dykes. Some of the older houses are still thatched but most are modern, often whitewashed or harled.

A mile to the north of Lybster, a road strikes out to the north-west through a shallow, green vale to Camster. Here, in the moorland beyond a small plantation of conifers, are to be found the Camster cairns. There are two: one is round with a single chamber, and the other is long and conceals in its innards at least two chambers. The cairns lie in the heather like two grey whales. Between four and five thousand years old, they were probably built in stages by the neolithic agricultural peoples who tilled the burn valleys. A saddle quern and pieces of undecorated, coarse pottery are among the finds from the cairns – scant clues to a vanished way of life. One flint arrowhead has also been found, and two pieces of pitchstone possibly originating on the Isle of Arran hint at ancient trade routes. The long cairn measures two hundred feet by sixty-five feet. The two chambers inside can be reached by crawling through low, narrow tunnels; a modern fanlight roof lets some light into the oval chambers which are perhaps ten feet across and are divided by large, vertical slabs. The round cairn, with one chamber, is fifty-five feet in diameter. The long cairn has a forecourt at either end, partly enclosed by curving horns of stone, a feature that leads one to speculate on their use as arenas for religious or social rituals. Chambered cairns in various shapes and sizes have been found over a wide area extending along the coast of Scotland from Kintyre north to Shetland, with the greatest concentration along the west side of the Moray Firth. As a reminder that building with stone is a long-persisting tradition, a circular sheep fank, probably built in the nineteenth century, stands between the two cairns at Camster.

Contemporary, or nearly so, with these immense tombs is another remarkable manifestation of the neolithic people's use of stone at the Hill o' Many Stanes at Mid Clyth. On this patch of moor, over two hundred flagstone boulders have been arranged in twenty-two almost parallel rows running north-south, covering an area of about sixty square yards. None of the stones rises more than a couple of feet from the heather and some are overgrown, but the whole arrangement is mysterious and impressive. Another series of stone rows, with at least one hundred stones, was found at Torrisdale in 1982 by an Ordnance Survey team.

To leap from prehistory to the 1980s by simply turning around is easy in Caithness and Sutherland. From the coast at Clyth the oil platforms of the Beatrice Oilfield are clearly visible. They stand about twelve miles offshore, like futuristic sea cities, brightly lit at night.

For a long time Caithness and Sutherland looked yearningly for some oil-related development. As the centres of the industry focused on Orkney, Shetland and Invergordon, many people felt that once again an economic opportunity had slipped through their fingers. A project to build an oil-platform repair yard at Dunnet fell by the wayside. Despite its central situation, labour force and harbour facilities, Wick could only look on as jobs and wealth flowed into Aberdeen. When the Beatrice field was discovered in 1976, hopes were high that its oil would be pumped ashore at, for example, Clyth Ness or Sinclair's Bay. In the event, a pipeline was laid to the Nigg terminal in Easter Ross, forty-nine miles away. The field has estimated reserves of 160 million barrels of high-wax oil. At low temperatures the crude is viscous; it starts to flow at 23°C. In 1983 Shell Oil announced that they were to begin test drilling north of the present field and closer inshore, only five miles from Clyth Ness. Some test drilling was done on land in the early 1980s, at Lothbeg, between Brora and Helmsdale, but the effort came to nothing.

Local conservationists are very conscious of the threat oil poses to the environment. The Moray Firth and its estuaries are important habitats for seabirds and fish, and monitoring of the effects of the new oil developments goes on continuously. The Royal Society for the Protection of Birds concluded a two-year survey in 1983. Aware of the adverse image created by such incidents as the wreck of the *Torrey Canyon* and of the ecological importance of the Firth, Britoil and its partners at Beatrice have established plans to control pollution. The waxy nature of the Beatrice oil makes the risk of a blow-out at the field a low one, but a spillage would pose a threat to the coast about twenty hours after the event. Emergency systems enable Beatrice to close down in thirty seconds, and elaborate operational procedures should ensure that no spillages occur.

Halberry Head is a great knuckle of rock protruding from the cliffs two miles north of the unmanned lighthouse at Clyth Ness. A deep geo divides it from its mother rock on the west side, leaving only a narrow isthmus, 150 feet across, as a bridge to the mainland. There is nothing but grass on it now but once it was crowned by a castle – the seat of George Gunn, the leader of his clan and the crowner or coroner of Caithness.

The office of crowner was established in the mid-fourteenth century by the Scots kings. The holders appear to have shared the government of particular areas with the sheriffs, the crowner being especially charged with inquests on murders, the arrest of persons openly accused of breaking the peace, and the levying of troops for the king's service. How the Gunns came to hold this office is obscure but in the mid-fifteenth century George Gunn was crowner and had earned the byname in Gaelic *Am Braisdeach Mor*, 'the big brooch', from the large silver ornament he wore to signify his position.

The Gunns are commonly held to be descended from the Norse, among whom 'Gunni' was a common name. One Gunni in particular is favoured with being the clan's progenitor – Gunni Andresson, the grandson of Svein Asleifarson whom we shall meet again in this book. Ian Grimble, however, considers the Gunns to be of Pictish origin 'especially in view of the inveterate hostility that continued for so many centuries between them and the Mackays, who were of Gaelic origin and had almost certainly invaded their neighbourhood in large numbers'. If this is the case, the word Gunn might be a relic of a pre-Celtic tongue.

To the north of Halberry Head, the A9 leaves the parish of Latheron and enters the parish of Wick. A mile north of the boundary, which passes close to the little kirk of Bruan on a bare braeside, is the small village of Ulbster and one of the most remarkable harbours built to exploit the herring shoals in the early nineteenth century – Whaligoe. The cove of Whaligoe is surrounded by high cliffs; at their base a platform, built up on some shelving rocks, has the ruins of an old storehouse. To reach this platform one has to descend a zigzagging staircase built into the cliff-face. Local tradition is that there were 365 steps, one for each day of the year; the actual number is less than this, but this does not detract from the feeling of exposure one gets during the descent, and it certainly did not make work greatly easier for the fishermen's wives who climbed the steps with creels of fish on their backs.

David Brodie of Hopeville, the tenant of this part of the Ulbster estate at the beginning of the nineteenth century, spent £53 on clearing the cove and building the platform, and £8 for the construction of the steps. When a storm threatened, the fishermen hauled their yawls up out of the sea on ropes and pulleys fixed to hooks in the cliff wall. By 1814 twenty-four boats were fishing from here, and it was still being used in the first half of this century.

Brodie is better remembered for laying out the village and fishing haven of Sarclet, about three miles north of Whaligoe and once called Brodiestown after its founder. The harbour here is wide, positively grand after the stormy confines of Whaligoe, and backed by a curving shingle beach. The old storehouses are still to be seen, though no boats fish from here now.

The A9 falls like a long, straight ribbon across the land from Ulbster north to Wick, passing through the village of Thrumster on the way. A prominent landmark here is the BBC relay mast, and running parallel with the road one can see the track of the old Lybster-Wick railway. The Lybster railway opened in 1903 and ran, slowly by all accounts, until April Fools' Day in 1944: one favourite joke was that a small boy stopped the train one day when he leaned out from the carriage to pluck a daisy from the embankment.

Wick is simply *vik*, the Norse for bay, and it seems to have been a centre of some importance since our earliest recorded history. There are few natural harbours in the rock wall that is the east coast of Caithness, and the mouth of the Wick river, with the stream itself threading a convenient route inland, would have been an attractive site. Vik is mentioned in the *Orkneyinga Saga* as being the residence of a farmer called Harold and as a place where the earls of Orkney sometimes resided. On the south side of the town is the ruin of Oldwick Castle, sometimes popularly called the Old Man o' Wick. 'The Old Man o' Wick was a man, when the Old Man o' Hoy was a boy', runs a local rhyme.

The castle is one of the oldest in Scotland: we know next to nothing of its early history, but it seems probable that it was here the earls of Orkney came, as the stonework places its age in the twelfth century. Like so many other fortresses in the north, it is built on a peninsula between two geos. The square keep, all that remains now, was once supplemented by a group of outbuildings and a courtyard. The keep rose to four storeys, each with a wooden floor resting on joists set into the walls; the main entrance was on the first floor and probably reached by a ladder, though the upper floors were served by a spiral staircase set into one corner of the building. There are no signs of chimneys, and the fireplace was probably in the centre of the floor, the smoke finding its own way out through ventholes and the narrow windows. In the fourteenth century the castle was occupied by a man of Norman descent, Sir Reginald de Cheyne, of whom more anon. Through the marriage of one of de Cheyne's daughters, it passed to the Sutherlands and later to the Oliphant family, who withstood a siege in it in 1569 until they had to surrender due to lack of water. The Oliphants sold it to the earls of Caithness, who passed it to the Campbells of Glenorchy in the mid-seventeenth century. The Dunbars of Hempriggs gained it from the Campbells, though it is likely that they did not inhabit it for long. Now it is in the care of the government.

Wick itself remained a small place throughout the Middle Ages. 'The chief towne in Caithness is called Wik,' wrote Bishop Leslie in 1578, 'ar lykwyse mony touris [towers] and sey portis [seaports] verie commodious.' Probably no more than a few straggling streets of wattle and turf houses, the town was sacked and burnt in 1588 by the forces of the Earl of Sutherland in another phase in the fluctuating feud between him and the house of Sinclair. On this particular occasion, the Sutherlands warmed up for their attack by pillaging the parish of Latheron before descending on Wick, in an unholy trinity with the Mackays of Strathnaver and the Macleods of Assynt. The Earl of Caithness retired to his stronghold at Girnigoe, leaving the invaders to torch the town. They spared the kirk, however, although one man broke open the lead casket that contained the heart of a former earl, looking for treasure but finding only dust.

Only a year later, the town became a royal burgh: a copy of the king's charter hangs in the hallway of the Town House. By the mid-seventeenth century the population was about five hundred. Trade seems to have been small, less than that enjoyed by Thurso. No archaeological work has been done to flesh out the bare outline we have of the town's early history, but recently the Scottish Burgh Survey has turned its attention to this problem.

The parish church, now at the west end of High Street, was in the Middle Ages at the other end of the town, but exactly where is unknown. The present church was built in about 1830 on the site of an older building dating to the sixteenth century. A fragment of that earlier church, known as the Sinclair aisle, remains, but repairs and ornamentation with crenellations in 1835 disguise its original character. At the foot of the brae near the church there used to be a well dedicated to the town's patron saint, Fergus.

The Market Square is the centre of the modern town, as it would have been of old, a swelling in the sinuous High Street, wider now than it once was, that runs along the north bank of the river to the sea's edge. The site of the old market cross is marked by stones set in the tarmac of the road close to the junction of High Street and Bridge Street. Tolbooth Lane indicates where the old town jail used to be, before it was replaced by the new Town House, with its cupola and clocks, and prison in Bridge Street in 1828.

The town is most famous for herring. Over one thousand boats used to crowd into the harbour in the nineteenth century during the annual two-month season. The population swelled to over ten thousand as workers came to catch and gut the fish. The museum run by the Wick Society in Bank Row near the harbour tells the story of these great years. This museum, the Wick Heritage Centre, opened its doors to the public in 1981 and is a splendid example of a community working together to conserve and present their history. The museum buildings date back to the early nineteenth century and contain a coopering yard, a smiddy and a fish-curing kiln; the exhibits cover all aspects of the herring industry.

In 1790 Thomas Telford inspected the north-east coast on behalf of the British Fisheries Society. He found small harbours at Keiss, Staxigoe, Dunbeath and a few other villages but, to provide proper facilities for the expansion of the herring fishery, he recommended the development of a harbour at Wick. The Society agreed and acquired a large tract of land in 1803 on the south side of the river, opposite the existing town. With grants from the government and funds raised elsewhere, the Society, with Telford as their guiding engineer, launched one of their most spectacular successes. The old wooden bridge over the river was demolished and replaced by a new stone one in 1808, built by a local man called George Burn to Telford's plans. Burn went on to build the harbour, which was completed in 1811 at a cost of £14,000. Telford planned a new village – streets, houses, warehouses and curing sheds – and the whole area was christened Pulteneytown after Sir William Pulteney, a governor of the British Fisheries Society who had died in 1805. Many of the older streets – Beaufoy, Huddart, Vansittart, Dempster – are named after members of the Society. To encourage growth, fishermen and coopers were granted houses free of rent for the first three years. By 1819 the population had reached two thousand. On a visit in 1825, Alexander Sutherland noted that, 'In every quarter carpenters' hammers were sounding ... and the boats, when finished, were to be borne to the beach on men's shoulders.' Boats began to come from other parts of Britain to take part in the lucrative herring fishery. By 1830 the resident population was being augmented by an influx of seven thousand workers during the season. Two hundred thousand barrels of fish were being exported every year. The harbour soon proved too small to cater for such a multitude: Telford planned an extension in 1823, and this was completed, after delays due to storm damage, in 1834.

The shoals of herring brought booming prosperity in their wake. 'To hear a Caithness man speak of the herring fishing,' commented Alexander Sutherland, 'one would suppose that it was the only guarantee Providence had given him that he should not perish by famine.' 'The silver darlings', to give the herring their fond nickname, spawned auxiliary industries: carting, curing, rope-making, chandlery, ship-building, net-making. From August through September, Wick was a heaving, bubbling cauldron of raucous activity. Men came to crew the boats from all over the north, and their wives, sisters and girl-friends came to gut, clean and pack the fish. Leaving Wick *en route* for Thurso in 1829, a traveller met groups of women 'all with golden tresses loose and uncombed, going to Wick to celebrate the first day of the herring fishery'.

The Reverend Charles Thomson claimed that, if the fishing was successful, not less than five hundred gallons of whisky would be drunk in a day; another minister complained that the new wealth was having 'pernicious effects upon the morals ... especially the young of both sexes'. Despite the fears of the clergy, the fishermen retained a strong sense of religion: among the features of this period of Wick's history were the large open-air church services held in and around the town, and several visitors commented on the habit of the fishermen of singing psalms at sea to pass the time before hauling the nets.

In the 1850s and '60s, the herring fleet reached its peak of over one thousand boats. When all were in harbour, one could cross dryshod from one pier to another. The itinerant workforce sought lodgings where they could find them, and sometimes ten or twelve could be accommodated in one room. The crowded, unsanitary conditions resulted in outbreaks of disease: 'Fever of a typhoid type is seldom absent from one lane or other,' said the minister in 1840, 'It is generally most acute soon after the close of the fishing season.' Smallpox and cholera also claimed their victims.

The herring fishing gave Wick its present shape and character. Telford's planned streets are still there, and the basins of his harbour. In 1836 the first issue of the *John O'Groat Journal* appeared; it has continued to appear since, every week, making it one of the oldest newspapers in Scotland. Robert Louis Stevenson came to the town in 1868 to learn to be a marine engineer like his father and grandfather, and stayed in a house in Harbour Terrace overlooking the bustle of the quays. This house is now the headquarters of HM Customs. Stevenson recalled this part of his life in an essay entitled *The Education of an Engineer*, in which he called Wick 'the meanest of man's towns, and situate certainly on the baldest of God's bays'. However disgruntled he was with his situation here, he was thrilled by the cliffs and the sea, and he went down into the water of the harbour in a diving suit and, some say, listened to stories from an old fisherman called Ben Gunn, whom he later immortalized in *Treasure Island*. Christopher Isherwood shared Stevenson's impressions in *Lions in Shadow*: he thought Wick 'a last outpost, a frontier fort against the savage, hostile sea'. Local people chuckle at such perversity; to me, as a child, Wick was south and very far from being a last outpost.

As the nineteenth century wore on to its close, the herring fishery slowly declined; the exact causes are obscure, but overfishing was probably one. Technological advances – the introduction of cotton instead of the heavier hemp for nets, the appearance of steam drifters – revitalized the industry periodically, but the long-term trend was downward. Herring fishing finally ceased at Wick in the 1950s, though an occasional shoal still turns up on the coast and sets the blood racing, and the feet sometimes, as it stirs old instincts.

A great deal of the flavour of life in the hectic years of the boom can be got from the remarkable photographs taken in and around Wick by the Johnstons – father, son and grandson – between 1863 and 1975. The father, Alexander Johnston, forsook a career as a clerk for the camera, and to him and his descendants we owe a priceless debt. The archive of thousands of Johnston negatives is now in the keeping of the Wick Society, and a selection has been published in Iain Sutherland's *Wick Harbour and the Herring Fishing.*

The town remains an important white-fishing port. Seine-net boats go far afield on week-long voyages that take them across the North Sea to Norway and Denmark, or west beyond Orkney as far as Rockall. The *Boy Andrew* holds the record for the largest seine-net catch in Scotland – 1,332 boxes (worth almost £59,000) taken in one week in January 1984. The weekly landings of cod, haddock, plaice, whiting and skate at Wick vary widely, but an approximate average is one thousand hundredweights. Modern boats such as the *Boy Andrew* are fully equipped with electronic aids but this should not lead the visitor into under-estimating the hard drag needed still to harvest the sea. Foreign vessels frequently call at Wick to land fish or seek replenishment of stores or repairs.

To many people, the name of Caithness is synonymous with glass – smoky-brown tumblers, elegant lilac vases or intricate paperweights. This is an indication of the success of an enterprise started by local businessmen in 1960. In the twenty-five years of its existence, Caithness Glass has become established as a name for excellence. Three Italian glass-blowers were involved in the firm's early days, setting up the factory and imparting their skills to local people. It is possible to visit the plant, to watch the glass-blowers with their long blowpipes handling blobs of molten glass with a temperature of over 1,000°C and skilfully shaping them into vases and glasses. One of the objects produced annually is the trophy for the BBC TV quizgame *Mastermind*.

Wick also has a distillery. Founded in 1826 by James Henderson, who is reputed to have been making whisky long before licensed to do so, the distillery produces the malt Old Pulteney. Another successful local business is Osprey Electronics. Since its founding in 1975, Osprey has grown to become one of the world's leading makers of underwater television and camera systems, exporting their electronic equipment worldwide as well as supplying the North Sea oil industry. The cameras are designed and manufactured in Wick, but in 1983 a branch operation opened in Aberdeen to handle sales and servicing. About fifty people are employed at the company's premises close to Wick Airport.

On the wall of a bank in High Street there is a plaque to the memory of Neil Gunn, bearing a quotation from his autobiography *The Atom of Delight* that sums up an important aspect of the northern way of life: 'In communal life it is quite simply the recognition of others, the need to be one with them and to enjoy the work and games, to contribute what one can to increase the mutual delight.'

Finally, before leaving Wick for other parts of Caithness, I must mention the statue of James T. Calder, the county's most famous historian. From his plinth, up on the brae behind the station-master's house, his effigy looks out across the river and through the sycamores towards the old town. His major work, *Sketch of the Civil and Traditional History of Caithness from the Tenth Century*, was first published in 1861. The second edition, of 1887, is still available as a facsimile, and I, no less than other writers, remain in his debt. The statue was put up in 1900 and is reputedly based on a sketch by John Nicolson, the Auckengill artist.

6

From Noss Head to Thurso

The stubby peninsula of Noss Head thrusts north-eastwards from Wick, bound by cliffs. On the seaward side, close to Wick, lie the two villages of Papigoe and Staxigoe. The former gets its name from the fact that priests once lived there; Staxigoe is called after the rock stack that rises near the shingle beach. The broad, square-shaped haven of Staxigoe was once a busy place: small schooners and smacks called here with salt, coal and iron and loaded meal and fish. Three men fitted out two sloops here in 1767 and sailed off to the herring fishing in Shetland: their enterprise marked the beginning of the great herring fishing at Wick. The present harbour at Staxigoe was constructed in 1830; by 1850 it was home to thirty-one boats. The village had its own private bank at one time, where, it is claimed, local currency was printed and used. Gradually, however, Staxigoe was eclipsed by Wick.

The road to Noss Head crosses the main runway at Wick Airport. The first air service in the area was established in 1933 by Captain E.E. Fresson, a former RFC pilot, and was called Highland Airways; it operated from grass runways at the farm of Hillhead on the south side of the town. The present airfield was constructed in 1939. During the Second World War it became a base for RAF Coastal Command. Today it is used by Loganair, Air Ecosse and other independent operators and has scheduled connections to Orkney, Inverness and Aberdeen.

A short distance west of the Noss Head lighthouse, built in 1849, where the cliffs curve round towards the sands of Sinclair's Bay, are the two castles of Girnigoe and Sinclair. Girnigoe is the more substantial ruin, rising in a sturdy keep from a narrow spit protected by geos on either side. The entrance to the castle passes through the tumbledown gables of Castle Sinclair (erected later than Girnigoe, in about 1606, and inhabited until about 1690) to a vaulted chamber. This dark room extends across the base of the Girnigoe tower to the inner courtyard. The remains of the spiral staircase to the first floor are clearly visible in one corner at the base of a turret. On the other side a large recess marks the kitchen fireplace, big enough to hold an ox, and a great chimney. In the south-west corner of the ground floor, steps lead down into a totally dark chamber, perhaps where the well was, and from the kitchen a passageway ends in a sheer drop overlooking the sea. There may have been a drawbridge across this chasm, allowing an alternative entrance to the kitchen. Out on the tip of the promontory, a rough flight of steps plunges through a tunnel to a natural landing place at the base of the cliff. The castle is inhabited only by seabirds now, and the sea surges all around it. Spare a thought for those who lived in this windy eyrie, more comfortable though it was than the huts common people had, and spare a bigger one for the masons who built it.

The Sinclairs emerged from a tangled skein of marriages and inheritances as the earls of Caithness in the mid-fifteenth century. As St Clairs they had appeared in Scotland in the reign of Malcolm Canmore, who gave them extensive lands in Midlothian. One of the line, Henry St Clair, was granted the earldom of Orkney in 1379, and it was his grandson William who became Earl of Caithness in 1455. The family had, however, been an important one in the north for some time before that; a Henry St Clair was 'ballivus' of Caithness in 1321.

The first Sinclair earl was succeeded by his son, also called William, in 1476. It was this William who fell at Flodden in 1513 and gave rise to the belief that it was unlucky for a Sinclair to cross the Ord on a Monday, the day the Earl had led his men south to join the royal army. Before his death, however, William had begun the building of the castle at Girnigoe. He married a daughter of the Keiths of Ackergill. In 1529 his grandson George became the fourth Earl. His was the longest, most bloody rule of any of his line. He must have been a powerful man, courageous, ruthless, fond of political intrigue, an absolute ruler, bound in plot and manoeuvre with the other nobles of the Scottish court.

For example, he was chancellor of the jury that in 1567 acquitted the Earl of Bothwell of the charge of the murder of Darnley, the husband of Mary, Queen of Scots, and later he signed a bond, along with John, Earl of Sutherland, as it happened, declaring Bothwell a fit husband for the widowed queen. In 1556 George was granted the justiciarship of Caithness, gaining the total power to condemn or pardon any crime except treason.

When the Earl of Sutherland and his wife were poisoned at Helmsdale in 1567, George took the Earl's son into his wardship and married him to his daughter Barbara. George has been suspected of being behind the murder of his neighbour, though this has never been proved, and it was to prevent a Sinclair take-over of the earldom of Sutherland that the Murrays of Dornoch persuaded the Sutherland heir to flee to Aberdeen. The consequence of this ploy – the sacking of Dornoch – has been recounted earlier.

When John Sinclair, George's son, refused to execute the hostages delivered up in the siege of Dornoch Cathedral and later went to live with the Chief of Mackay in Strathnaver, George smelled a plot. Perhaps the son was conspiring to overthrow the father: we have no way of knowing, because George took drastic action and put an end to the business. He sent messengers to his son to express a desire for reconciliation but, when his son came to Girnigoe, he seized him and threw him into a dungeon. Here the hapless youth lingered for six years before, so goes the story, he was fed salt beef and left to die of thirst on 15 March 1576.

George Sinclair died in Edinburgh in September 1582 and was buried in the St Clair chapel at Roslin in Midlothian. His heart was removed from his body and taken north in a casket of lead to Wick church, where what was left of it was scattered to the winds by a Sutherland raider during the sack of Wick in 1588.

The A9 leaves Wick in a north-westward direction across the Caithness plain. A mile from the town, the B874 branches off and follows the course of the Wick river. In a field between the road and the river, on the crest of a brae beside a small ravine, stands a Celtic cross: the burn flowing down through the ravine is called the Altimarlach, possibly derived from the Gaelic *Allt na Meirleich* 'the stream of the thief', and it gave its name to the last major clan battle fought in Scotland.

The conflict took place between the Sinclairs and the

Campbells of Glenorchy. The sixth Earl of Caithness died in 1676 without a male heir; during his life, he had accrued enormous debts and had made a deposition in favour of Ian Campbell of Glenorchy, surrendering his earldom in return for financial help. After the Earl's death, however, George Sinclair of Keiss disputed Glenorchy's right to the title and lands of Caithness; preferring one of their own, the other Caithness lairds supported him. The upshot of the dispute was that Glenorchy led a small army of seven hundred north to fight for his rights, in the summer of 1680. Sinclair hastily scraped together a force to meet this invasion. The two armies encountered each other at dusk on 12 July at Stirkoke, on the south side of the river; but it was too late in the day to fight. Campbell took his men off to spend the night on the Hill of Yarrows, while Sinclair's force withdrew to Wick.

There is a story that Glenorchy arranged for a copious supply of whisky to be available to his opponents that night, by having a ship laden with it wreck itself on the Wick coast. It is also possible that Glenorchy paid unscrupulous smugglers, already with barrels of moonshine in their cellars, to broach them for the brave local lads. When morning came, and the Campbells rose from their plaids ready for battle, Sinclair's untried force was struggling from the fog of a hangover. Glenorchy's men crossed the Wick river and took up a position at Altimarlach, where they divided their force between the open riverside and the ravine. The Caithness men were drawn into a trap and utterly defeated: Sinclair himself and his mounted men were able to cut their way to safety, but perhaps two hundred of his followers fell.

The pipe tune 'The Campbells Are Coming' was composed on the occasion of this battle, and the tune 'The Carles Wi' the Breeks', a reference to the fact that Caithness men wore breeches instead of kilts.

Glenorchy remained Earl of Caithness for six years, during which time his tenants continually rebelled against him, burning his corn, robbing his factors, hamstringing his cattle. George Sinclair besieged and took Sinclair Castle, an act for which he was outlawed and later pardoned; and eventually he succeeded in gaining the title to the earldom. Glenorchy was given the barony of Wick and the earldom of Breadalbane in compensation.

Ackergill Tower is easily spotted from the A9. The seventy-foot tower dominates the shoreline of Sinclair's Bay. Although the road down to it is closed and overgrown, one can walk around the beach from the little village of Ackergill to view it from the sea side. The tower probably dates originally from the fifteenth-century; the sloping-roofed structure on the top and various other alterations were added or made in 1851, to plans by the architect David Bryce. The tower is still inhabited and is the seat of the Dunbar family of Hempriggs.

In 1538 the castle and half the lands of Ackergill were granted by James V to William, Earl Marischal, and Lady Margaret Keith, his wife. The Keiths were a very powerful family, and with the headquarters of their power only two miles along the shore from Girnigoe it was perhaps inevitable that conflict between them and the Sinclairs should erupt. In 1547 George Sinclair grabbed Alexander Keith and his servant, John Skarlet, and held them against their will; and in 1556 the Earl of Caithness besieged the Keiths at Ackergill.

At Reiss, slightly over a mile beyond Ackergill, the A9 makes a sharp right-angled bend to the north; the junction is better known locally as Plover Inn. The B876 runs on past the old runways and crumbling blockhouses of the Second World War aerodrome of Skitten to the low-lying Killimster Moss. A chapel dedicated to St Duthac once stood here, and the area was probably the site of one of the early battles between the invading Norse and the indigenous Celts towards the end of the tenth century.

The story of the battle is told like a legend in the *Orkneyinga Saga*. The Norse jarl Sigurd Hlodvisson was challenged to battle at Skitten by one Finnleik, mormaor of Moray. A cautious man, Sigurd sought the advice of his mother. Her reply – that if she had suspected that her son wanted to live for ever, she would have raised him in her wool basket – was probably not what he wanted to hear. But the redoubtable lady gave him a banner that would guarantee him victory but which would bring death to whoever bore it. The magical banner resembled a raven flying and, true enough, although Sigurd was victorious in the conflict with Finnleik, three standard-bearers, in turn carrying the raven, were killed.

From Reiss, the A9 descends gently to the valley of the burn of Wester. Like many miles of road in the north-east of Caithness, it follows a straight course; on the right the traveller can see Reiss golf course laid out on the sandy pasture behind the rampart of sand dunes that flanks the long beach of Sinclair's Bay. The road crosses the sluggish, winding Wester on a new bridge, just downstream from its hump-backed predecessor that dates from the early nineteenth century. Between the two bridges runs a railway track, laid arrow-straight across the links. At the seaward end of the track stand the sheds and plant of Kestrel Marine Ltd. This company set up its base in Wick in 1978 and began operations at Wester constructing pipelines for the offshore oilfields. As the sections of pipe are welded together, the whole line moves inland along the railway track. Completed pipes are floated off, pulled into the sea by specially equipped barges, and towed to the oilfields.

Just beyond the Wester, a road turns off to the west to the district of Lyth. In the old school here, the Lyth Arts Society, formed in 1977, runs an arts centre, the only one in the county. The gallery, which mounts exhibitions of contemporary art, can be converted into a studio-theatre to accommodate an audience of eighty. Touring companies put on performances between exhibitions. The centre closes down in winter but in summer it is a lively place, much visited by tourists and school parties. It is also the headquarters of the Caithness Workshops Guild of Artist-Craftsmen, an umbrella organization for the various independent craftspeople in the area.

The village of Keiss takes its name from the Norse word for a ridge of land, an appropriate derivation for the rows of houses stretching along the spine of ground between the A9, two miles north of Wester, and the little harbour nestling at the foot of precipitous braes. As a village, Keiss owes its origins to the herring fishing, but in this century it is more famous as a centre for crab fishing. In 1976 the three boats working here landed over thirty-two metric tons of shellfish, worth almost £20,000. A local fisherman has praised the sea's harvest in verse:

> The wind is blowan frae the East,
> It's been there now a month at least;
> A'm thinkan o' ma favourite feast,
>   A good Keiss partan.*

* 'Partan' is the Caithness dialect for crab.

'A steak is better,' some folks boast,
There's some prefer a lump o' roast;
There's others sit and nibble toast,
    Gie me a partan.

The creels used in Keiss, as elsewhere in the Highlands and islands, differ from the circular lobsterpots which are probably more familiar to English visitors. The creel is rectangular, traditionally made from netting stretched over a wood and hoop frame though nowadays cast entirely in plastic or with a metal frame. Each creel contains a heavy stone to act as a sinker, attached to which is an arrangement of cords to hold the bait in place. The best bait is held to be skate. Two funnels, called monkeys, are woven into the sides of the creel to allow the crabs and lobsters to enter but not to escape. Each boat fishes with about one hundred creels, arranged in flights or 'flychers' of about twenty; each day the creels are hauled up, relieved of their catch, rebaited and cast back into the sea.

At Stain, just to the south of Keiss on the shore, James Bremner was born in 1784. A monument in the form of a tall obelisk stands overlooking Wick harbour to the memory of this remarkable salvage expert and marine engineer. He built many of the harbours around the north-east coast, including the one in his native village, which he began in 1818. The back of the north quay at Keiss is a good example of the technique he developed whereby the blocks of stone are laid vertically so that the explosive power of the surf is harmlessly dissipated along the crevices between them. Bremner rescued or salvaged hundreds of vessels that came to grief on his stormy native coast, showing an ingenuity and heroism that led him eventually to be the man who saved Brunel's *Great Britain* when she went aground in Ireland in 1846. Bremner's activities, which included ship-building, made him a wealthy man but to the end of his days he kept his generosity and openhandedness, particularly towards shipwrecked mariners.

North of the village stand the two castles of Keiss. The older, now a ruin, dates from the late sixteenth century and rears up from the cliffhead at Fulligoe as if the masonry grew naturally from the rock. The newer castle, a white-painted mansion, was built in the mid-eighteenth century and is still occupied, though not by the Sinclairs who were the original lairds but by an American businessman. Beyond the castles, the A9 curves around the broad headland of Nybster, or the Dog's Nose as it is more commonly known 'because it is always cold and wet'. On the point of Nybster is the site of the oldest Baptist church in Scotland. Sir William Sinclair of Keiss was converted to Baptism in the 1750s: for a time he preached to his tenants in a room in the castle, and he remained a pastor for fourteen years. The present church was built in 1856.

There are the remains of several brochs along this stretch of coast, by the sea and beside the cemetery at Keiss, and at Auckengill, where some bear the elaborate additions of John Nicolson. This amateur antiquarian, artist and sculptor was born at Stempster near John o'Groats in 1843; he died in 1934 after a lifetime of academic and artistic endeavour. He painted local scenes and characters, investigated the history and genealogy of the region, made clay pipes from local clay, designed and carved tombstones, and helped Sir Francis Tress Barry, the proprietor of Keiss Castle, excavate the local brochs in the 1890s, as well as carrying on the farming of his land. Some of his carvings decorate the walls of his house at Auckengill, and the old school here has been converted into a museum celebrating his achievements.

The A9 leaves the vale of Auckengill by a steep hill to cross a ridge of moor to Freswick. A glance seaward at the crest of the ridge will catch the ruin of Buchollie Castle, which occupies the top of a sea stack at the edge of the cliffs. The ruins date from the fourteenth century, when the Mowat family from Buchollie in Aberdeenshire received a grant of land at Freswick from Robert the Bruce. The estate was sold to the Sinclairs in the seventeenth century, and it is probable that the castle was abandoned at that time. It is a wild, windy spot, seeming more exposed than many of the Caithness castles that are built on similar sites; it is believed to be the site of Lambaborg, a fortress built at Freswick by Svein Asleifarson in the twelfth century.

The valley of Freswick is a green bowl between the moors and the sea. The tall tower of Freswick House, which dates from the seventeenth century and was probably begun by the Sinclairs after they acquired the land from the Mowats, dominates the scene. On a wet day the tower looks grey and forbidding and seems to invite its nickname of 'the house of cruelty', reputedly earned because of the labour the tenants of the estates had to contribute to build it, though an alternative source might have been the rack-renting imposed by the lairds in the eighteenth century. A small cell for punishing locals who offended the laird still exists in the bridge across the burn close to the tower. There is also a fine example of an eighteenth-century doocot (dovecot) here.

Freswick, in its original Norse form of Thrasvik, is mentioned in the *Orkneyinga Saga* but, although its association with the Norse settlement of Caithness has been known for a long time, it was only in 1980 that archaeologists, from Durham University, began extensive research in the sand dunes at the head of the bay. Objects from earlier digs in the 1930s and '40s are on display at the National Museum of Antiquities in Edinburgh. The dunes have been heavily used during the centuries and have suffered erosion, but excavations have uncovered houses, a smiddy and a bath-house as well as pottery, quernstones and a thirteenth-century English coin. Middens of kitchen refuse have yielded up large quantities of shell and fishbones. In 1981 a longhouse was discovered, the only mainland Scottish site for such a find.

According to *Orkneyinga Saga*, which was probably written early in the thirteenth century in Iceland, Freswick was part of the lands belonging to Svein Asleifarson. The exploits of this colourful character dominate the later sections of the *Saga*. He was a Viking of a kind that was already becoming obsolete in his day. As well as Freswick, he held the island of Gairsay in Orkney, where he had a great longhouse and kept an armed retinue: it was his custom to spend the winter at this base and then in spring and autumn sally out raiding and pillaging around the coasts of Britain. As mentioned before, he fortified Lambaborg. He met his end very much as he had lived – by the sword – probably in 1171 in Dublin. The *Saga* describes Svein's death only, but Irish sources record that in that year the deposed King of Dublin was defeated while attacking the city with the help of a fleet from Orkney.

The last few miles of the A9 wind over the Warth Hill and offer to the traveller the splendid prospect of the Pentland Firth and the islands of Orkney, before the road drops down to John o'Groats and comes to a stop at the edge of the sea.

John o'Groats has been a destination for centuries. Early writers refer to it as the most northerly extremity of mainland Britain: it isn't, this honour belonging to Dunnet Head a few miles to the west, but as the opposite corner of the country to Land's End in Cornwall, John o'Groats has seen the start or finish of many a strange journey. Some visitors have confessed to a disappointment with the place, seeing only a clutch of unremarkable houses, a car-park and bad weather. They have missed what John o'Groats has to offer: the white beach of Sannick, the cliffs and stacks around Duncansby Head, and the clear, enchanting light of the northern summer. The latter won over the normally scathing and pompous Alexander Sutherland in 1825: 'The beams of the declining sun, as it hung in glory over the broad Atlantic, played with the brilliancy of a tropic summer,' he enthused in his journal.

Duncansby is the older name: Duncan or Dungal was a local Celtic mormaor whose name the Norse gave to the district. As 'Dungesbi', it appears on the first sea-chart of the Atlantic to be drawn by copper-plate engraving by Italian cartographers in 1569. In the fifteenth century another visitor came to stay and gave his name to the village. Jan de Groot and his two brothers, Malcolm and Gavin, were granted a charter by the king of Scots to operate a ferry from here to Orkney. De Groot was a Dutchman, or at least of Dutch descent, for his brothers' Celtic names indicate that the family may have been resident in Scotland for some time. He and his descendants grew wealthy and numerous, and it was their custom to foregather annually in Jan's house to celebrate their arrival in Caithness. One year, a tremendous quarrel over precedence, almost resulting in bloodshed, broke out among the sons. Jan quietened them and promised that before the next gathering he would solve the problem. He built an octagonal house with eight doors, containing an octagonal table – one side for himself and for each of his prickly offspring. This, at least, is the story, the first written version of which appears in the *Statistical Account* of the parish published in the 1790s. The octagonal house became an item on the itinerary of travellers in the eighteenth century, by which time it was no more than a mound of stones and grass – 'a ruine', said Bishop Forbes in 1762. The site of the house is marked by a flagpole today, but its shape is commemorated in the plan of the John o'Groats House Hotel nearby and in the wooden souvenir shop at the harbour. In the summer months a ferry runs from John o'Groats to South Ronaldsay, along the route old Jan would have taken.

The shell sands along the beach here are derived from deepwater molluscs as well as inshore species. The most famous shell is a delicate, tiny cowrie, known locally as a groatie buckie, but it is difficult to find. Searching for them used to be a childhood pursuit, and many croft kitchens had a carefully gleaned jarful of these shells. In 1700 John Brand found the people using them to make necklaces, and a boy tried to sell some to Bishop Forbes on his visit.

The name of the Pentland Firth is Norse – from Pettalandsfjörthr, 'the strait of the land of the Picts' – and it is one of the roughest, most treacherous patches of ocean in the world. Through the seven-mile-wide channel, the tide races between the Atlantic and the North Sea at speeds surpassing ten knots, a force sufficient in the days of sail to drive a ship backwards against the wind. Captains preferred to take a longer route north around Orkney rather than attempt the roosts, eddies and whirlpools of the Firth, some of which bear colourful names – the Men o'Mey, the Bores o'Duncansby, the Swelkie.

The main channel for shipping passes through the Outer Sound, between Swona and Stroma, two islands sitting astride the turbulent streams. The eastern gateway to the Firth is marked by a group of rocky islets, the Pentland Skerries, which are a part of the Orkney parish of South Ronaldsay. The lighthouse on the Skerries dates from 1794 and is one of many built by Robert Louis Stevenson's grandfather.

The Swelkie is named from the Norse *svelgr*, 'whirlpool', and that is exactly what it is. It forms like a whirling pit in the sea off the north-east tip of Stroma at certain stages of the tide. According to Norse legend, it is the place where a magic quernstone sank after the sea-king Mysing ordered it to grind out salt. Mysing had stolen the stone from its rightful owner, for whom it could grind anything required, but in his haste neglected to find out how to stop it. While passing through the Firth, Mysing wanted some salt for his food, commanded the stone to produce some and then sank to his doom as his ship piled up with salt from the uncontrollable magic quern. The stone still grinds, pouring salt into the ocean, and the sea roars around it.

In the 1740s, the first proper survey of the Firth was carried out by an Orkneyman, Murdoch Mackenzie, who incidentally was the first to use the modern method of triangulation in map-making. Mackenzie's charts were published in 1750, and in the decades thereafter shipping began to use the Firth to a much greater extent than before. Further surveys were made by the Admiralty in the nineteenth century, but some parts of the Firth remain to be adequately charted.

Despite the charts, a lighthouse and better-equipped ships, mariners found the Firth still a kittle beast. It was the custom for a ship in need of a pilot to signal as she approached the Firth and to pick up a local man. Piloting was an exciting, dangerous business. Some pilots found themselves being borne to England or North America by captains unwilling to shorten sail to let them leave the ship after the Firth was safely astern. For this reason, pilots usually went out with companions, who were then taken in tow in their yawl behind the ship. For a single passage of the Firth, the pilot normally received about one guinea, although payment was frequently in the form of duty-free tobacco, liquor or goods. Quite often captains gave promissory notes to pilots so that later they could claim payment from the ships' owners, a business that frequently took a long time to settle.

The stories about the pilots show them to have been a tough breed. James Mowat of Skirza took one ship west through the Firth in 1870 while still wearing his carpet slippers; in his haste to be the first pilot to reach the ship, he had risen from his fireside as he was, and he ended up in Quebec. Pilots lost their lives. One incident will serve to commemorate the many who were drowned. In April 1848 six men went out from Duncansby to a west-bound ship, the *William Gouland* of Sunderland. As usual one man went aboard as pilot and the other five stayed in their yawl which was taken in tow. But the strong north-easterly breeze broke the towrope and threw the yawl against the ship's stern. The five occupants were spilled into the sea and, despite efforts to save them, lost: they included a man and his eldest son, and two brothers.

The cliffs at Duncansby show the range of sculpture that the sea can carve in rock. To the west of the lighthouse there is the Glupe, where the waves have drilled a tunnel into the rock at sea-level and blasted an opening upwards to the sky. With great care, one can walk around the Glupe, crossing the natural bridge at the seaward side, and peer into the gloomy, dank cavern. In storm weather spray drifts up from the hole like steam from a pot.

Between the Glupe and the lighthouse is Longgeo, whose sides are sheer walls crowded with raucous birds. The Long Geo of Slaites to the south of the lighthouse is more spectacular still. The slightest sufferer from vertigo should approach its edge with care, though there is a fence which makes a walk safe, for the walls of the geo fall two hundred feet with a slight overhang to deep, green sea sucking and surging far below. The guillemots clustered on ledges at sea-level look tiny in the distance.

From the outermost point at the south side of the geo, one can see Humlies Hole, a stack in the making. The sea has carved away a pillar of rock from the cliff, leaving the stack connected by a fragile-looking bridge to the land behind. One day, this sandstone umbilicus will be cut and another stack will stand clear from the parent rock.

Two stacks, the Knee and Gibb's Craig, lie to the south. Between the Knee and the main cliff the sea froths in a tidal race called the Rispie. Further south still, the cliff drops to modest proportions before rising again towards the three Stacks of Duncansby. One can descend to the shingle beach here and scramble through the Thirl Door – a hole through the cliff and another stack in the making. The three Stacks are called the Muckle Stack, the Peedie (little) Stack and the Tom Thumb Stack, in order of size; the Muckle Stack is almost three hundred feet high. Samuel Lewis described them in 1846 as shooting up 'fantastically to a great height, attracting, in the spring and summer, swarms of sea-fowl, and on the top of the larger stack, the eagle has its habitation'. He may have been referring to a sea-eagle, but alas they are no longer here. The seafowl still swarm – gannets, fulmars, cormorants, seaducks, skuas, guillemots, puffins and gulls – for this is a fertile sea, and the John o'Groats fishermen set their creels close in to the cliff.

Needless to say, exploration of this coastline should be undertaken with care, and with attention to local advice.

From John o'Groats the A836 runs west along the coast. Half a mile from John o'Groats it passes the old mill at Huna, the only water-powered mill still in operation in the north. Although there has probably been a mill on this site since Norse times, the present building dates from 1901, and some of the working parts of the mill are of the same age. In recent years there has happily been an increasing demand for meal ground in the traditional manner.

Until the establishment of the steamer crossing between Scrabster and Orkney in the 1850s, Huna was the southern terminus of the main ferry to the islands. Huna Inn was a famous, or rather notorious, hostelry where travellers could be storm-bound for days in doubtful comfort. In the early nineteenth century the mailboat crossed the Firth twice a week and carried passengers at the single fare of nine shillings.

The southern shore of the Firth is rocky but not of any great height; the ebbing tide leaves bare a wide curve of weed and stone in Gills Bay, where seals are fond of hauling themselves ashore to bask. Canisbay kirk, a prominent building, sturdy and white, dates from before the Reformation. A red stone slab, reputed to be the tombstone of Jan de Groot, used to stand in the churchyard but now it is kept inside the church to thwart the erosive power of the rain; the inscription, in cramped letters, begins: 'DONALD GROT, SONE OF IHONE GROT, LAID ME HER ....'

To the west of Gills Bay the land runs out to form St John's Point. The cliffs on this promontory rise almost to one hundred feet and guard a lovely, oval creek, almost completely enclosed and invisible except when one is standing above it, called Scotland's Haven. The headland also bears the marks of an ancient fort: the traces of an artificial ditch run across it, and the remains of middens have been found in association with it.

The road climbs up from Gills Bay to pass over to Mey, and from the crest of the brae there is a fine view of Stroma. The most northern part of Caithness and the county's only island, Stroma is now uninhabited but until the mid 1950s it had a resident population. The name means 'the island in the tide' and was bestowed on the island by the Norse, who established a permanent population here, perhaps intermarrying with Picts in the process, in the ninth or tenth centuries. On the south-west tip near Mell Head, there are the remains of a castle called Mestag about which hardly anything is known but which probably dates from the twelfth century. The island became a part of Caithness, according to legend, when snakes were brought there to settle a dispute between the earls of Orkney and Caithness over who was the rightful overlord. There are no snakes in Orkney; and so, when the snakes on Stroma lived, the island was judged properly to be a part of the mainland. In the seventeenth century it became the property of a Kennedy family, one of whom is said to have fled here to avoid retribution after he killed an opponent in a duel. The Kennedys laid their dead in a vault where the salt air inhibited the decomposition of the corpses, a phenomenon that excited considerable curiosity among the travellers of the time. The small square keep of the vault can still be seen on the eastmost corner of the island.

Stroma is a place of the sea. The men fished the Firth and acquired a high reputation as pilots and boatbuilders. We shall never know how many ships and lives have come to an end on Stroma's shores or in the surrounding waters, but notices such as the one in *Lloyd's List* on 3 December 1790 that the *Elizabeth and Mary* bound from Narva to Liverpool was 'on shore on the island of Stromay. Crew lost' were frequent. In the nineteenth century the island also had a reputation as a centre for smuggling and moonshining. The authorities were driven to great lengths to outwit the canny law-breakers, and raids were carried out in foggy weather when their approach could go undetected.

The lighthouse at the north end of the island was built in 1890. At that time the population was still around four hundred, but by 1949 it had fallen to ninety. As young folk left to seek a better life on the mainland or abroad, the old people felt driven to follow them. A new harbour was built on the south side in the 1950s but this failed to turn around the exodus. Stroma now belongs to one farmer who lives at Gills and who commutes to his estate in the Firth by boat.

When the tide is flowing east, an infamous race called the Men o'Mey forms off St John's Point and at its maximum extent creates a barrier right across the Firth to Tor Ness on Hoy that can be two miles wide with breakers rearing forty feet into the air. When a westerly or north-westerly gale is blowing, the

Admiralty cautions that 'the extreme violence' of the sea 'can hardly be exaggerated'. John Brand, who crossed the Firth at the end of the seventeenth century, wrote of the Men in tones which every later commentator has echoed: 'The leaping and danceing, as it were, of the waters there, tho Mirth and Danceing be far from the minds of the Seamen and Passengers who shall be so unhappy as to fall in among them, especially when any Sea is going.'

From the Caithness coast one can also see the flare of gas burning perpetually at the oil centre on Flotta. Large oil-tankers come in to load here and, needless to say, their passage through such dangerous waters is not of little concern.

From the gentle summit of Mey Hill, with its fine view of Dunnet Head, crouching like a massive sleeping lion to the west, the A836 runs down to Mey itself. To the north side of the plantation that straggles along the road stands the Castle of Mey, a favourite residence of the Queen Mother. The castle, at various times called Barrogill Castle, is a late-sixteenth century building with some nineteenth-century modifications; its construction probably began in about 1567, after the fourth Earl of Caithness acquired the lands of Mey from the Bishop of Caithness. William Daniell made an aquatint of the castle in 1813 which shows a solid, plain tower with riders cantering through a garden where, forty years before, Bishop Forbes found a fine crop of apples, strawberries and cherries. The Queen Mother bought the Castle of Mey in 1952. Since then extensive renovations have turned it into a comfortable mansion house, and the gardens are open to the public on certain dates.

The A836 passes through the village of Mey and continues westward across a low-lying stretch of bog. A secondary road follows the coastline through the districts of Harrow, Scarfskerry and Rattar. The cliffs along this section of the shore rarely rise above thirty feet, and small harbours nestle in the larger creeks. Phillip's Harbour at Harrow was built originally in the early nineteenth century but it was restored and reopened only a few years ago; someone has sketched the outlines of trawlers and seine-net boats in the concrete of the new harbour wall, likely to be the closest this small harbour will ever get to seeing these large fishing vessels. The most interesting feature is the buildings that formed part of a flagstone works which were started in 1872. Over fifty men worked here once, cutting, polishing and transporting the stone, and a light railway ran from the works to the quay with cargo for the schooners.

The coast road runs through the village of Scarfskerry – the name means 'the rock of the cormorant' – where the houses are strung out like beads on a necklace. Behind the houses and the parks of the crofts one can see the shallow, marshy Loch of Mey, and among twisted, sharply dipping rocks to the west of Scarfskerry Point lies the little harbour called simply 'The Haven'. This was the terminus for the other Caithness ferry to Orkney: two boats were involved, a large one to carry horses and cattle, and a small one for human passengers. The cross-Firth traffic in horses was quite heavy, some three hundred animals making the journey in each direction every year at the beginning of the nineteenth century. The fare was then three to four shillings for a horse, and a guinea for a person.

West of Scarfskerry the A836 runs past the Hill of Barrock through Corsback to Dunnet, but again this section is supplemented by a longer but more interesting stretch of secondary road along the coast.

The old harbour at Ham, build by James Traill of Castletown during the Age of Improvement, is now in a ruinous state but is still an impressive example of flagstone building. There is also an old mill here, where the road makes a sharp double bend before crossing the burn and climbing up past the farm of Ham. The road leads round to the village of Brough, where there is a pier and a seastack that can be reached at low tide.

From Brough the B855 runs up to Dunnet Head, the most northerly point of the British mainland, a great fist of heather and sandstone, in effect a moorland plateau with lochs crouching in folds in the ground and girt about with a red cliff wall. The road ends at the lighthouse. Built in 1831, the lantern in the tower is 346 feet above sea-level and in clear weather can be seen for twenty-four miles.

Facing Dunnet Head across the Firth are the red cliffs of Hoy, and the two walls of rock make an impressive gateway for ships passing to and from the Atlantic. The point with the lighthouse is called Easter Head on Ordnance Survey maps but this name is hardly ever used locally, Dunnet Head being applied to serve in its place. On old maps a name now extinct is given – Quinicnap or Whinynap (the spelling varies greatly). This word is taken to refer to the quern-like shape of the promontory when viewed from the east, although George Watson has suggested a derivation from two Norse words *kvi* and *knappr*, meaning in combination 'the folds at the head'.

The road from Brough to the village of Dunnet skirts St John's Loch. Noted now for the quality of its trout, the fame of this broad water once rested on its supposed healing properties. Invalids used to come here on the first Monday of certain months, walk around the loch, bathe in it, throw in some money and try to be out of sight of the water by the following sunrise. This practice and others persisted into the beginning of the nineteenth century, perhaps relics of the pre-Reformation Catholic faith or of an older, pre-Christian religion. Of the pilgrimage to the loch, the parish minister observed wryly: 'Hypochondriacs and nervous people may sometimes feel better after this ... but those seriously ill are of course the worse for it, and die occasionally by the road.'

The village of Dunnet, at the north-east corner of Dunnet Bay, has grown considerably in recent years as new houses have been built at the crossroads where the B855 joins the A836, and it no longer deserves the description afforded in 1829 by one traveller of 'a cluster of houses around a huge belfryed barn'. The 'barn' is the handsome white church, most of which dates from before the Reformation, the north aisle having been added in 1837. One of the parish ministers here was Timothy Pont, the grandson of a Venetian Protestant who emigrated to Scotland in the sixteenth century. Pont was a minister from 1601 to about 1614 (the date of his resignation is uncertain). He walked over most of the north, gathering information for the maps that are his chief memorial. When he died, the work was taken over and completed by Robert Gordon of Straloch, and the maps were published in 1668 in Amsterdam as part of Blaeu's atlas of Europe.

To the west of the village the land rises in a great wave to form Dwarwick Head. At the foot of the Head is a small pier where a monument commemorates a landing by the royal family in 1953, and under the cliffs is a cave where a mermaid once imprisoned her unfaithful human lover. From Dwarwick Head low reddish cliffs extend round to the beginning of the wide sweep of sand that makes Dunnet beach one of the finest in the north. At the base of the low cliffs there is a rock, marked with the print of a foot, knee and fingers, where the Devil landed when he once jumped across the bay from Castletown. The sandy beach is used for sand-yachting and, in the past, when low tide exposed the great width of firm sand, it served as a road for travellers. The dunes that back the beach and hide it from the A836 have been planted in places with conifers which, with the acres of marram grass, 'bent' in local speech, attempt to prevent the fierce westerly gales from blasting sand inland.

The boundary between the parishes of Dunnet and Olrig reaches the sea half-way along the sands. Olrig, under its landlord James Traill (1758–1847), was among the first parishes in Caithness to show the results of agricultural improvement. Flax was grown here for a linen manufactory, and Traill planted several acres of trees around his home at Castlehill; the woods are much neglected now, and the big house at Castlehill was ruined by a fire a few years ago. Son of the parish minister at Dunnet, Traill gained his estates by marrying the daughter of the Earl of Caithness. He was an energetic, far-sighted man and, although he forced twenty crofters to quit their land when he opened Inkstack quarry, he seems on the whole to have been a benevolent landlord. His major work was the opening of flagstone quarries at Castletown.

After a slow start this industry grew into one of great local importance, by the end of the nineteenth century employing about five hundred men. Castlehill harbour was built to provide a haven for the schooners that came to load up with dressed stone. The first shipment took place in April 1825. The quarries were connected with the harbour by a bogie track along which horses pulled the loads of stone. Quarry workers were given plots of ground on favourable terms, and the village of Castletown grew quickly into the mile-long settlement it is today; Alexander Sutherland thought it 'the seat of industry and intelligence'. (Some of these qualities persist: in 1983 the local firm of Norfrost Ltd, which employs over eighty people to manufacture domestic freezers, won the Lloyds Bowmaker award for industrial achievement.) Caithness flagstone has great strength and was much sought after for paving stone. The Royal Society of Arts tested the stone in 1849 and found that a three-inch thickness could support a weight over three thousand pounds. Over a hundred towns in Britain and the Empire used it to pave their streets; in the streets of Chelsea, one can still walk on Caithness flags laid last century.

At the beginning of this century the industry went into decline and has never recovered, its product unable to compete with concrete, although in 1949 a quarry at Spittal reopened to provide stone for special purposes such as fireplace facings. The big quarries at Castletown are likely to be brought out of the neglect in which they have languished for decades as some local people have recently formed a heritage society which intends to use them as the centrepiece of a museum to mark their history.

From Castletown the A836 runs west through Murkle, a broad, shallow valley of fields and farms. A small beach crouches beside the point called the Spur, the most prominent feature on this stretch of low, rocky coast. The hill of Clardon divides the expanse of Thurso Bay from Murkle. Near its summit stands a little castellated structure known as Harald's Tower, built by Sir John Sinclair, who thought it 'a considerable ornament to the neighbourhood', as a burial vault for the Ulbster family. Traditionally this is the site of a battle between the Norse earls and the Scots at the end of the twelfth century. Harald Maddadarson was Earl of Orkney and part of Caithness at the time: after being granted the title at the age of five, he ruled his domain jointly or singly for sixty-eight winters, according to the *Orkneyinga Saga*, and survived several attempts on his life and position. Through marriage, he allied himself with the Celtic house of Moray which swung between open and covert conflict with the kings of Scotland. William the Lion, King of Scots from 1165 to 1214, was continually preoccupied with this northern threat, and he tried to place a Norseman called Harald Ungi, or 'the Young' to distinguish him from Maddadarson, in the earldom of Caithness. The ageing Harald refused to accept the King's proposal and sent the royal messengers away with burning ears. Harald Ungi came north with an army but Harald Maddadarson routed the invaders on the braes of Clardon (though some claim that the battle was fought closer to Wick). Harald Ungi fell. On the night after he was killed, a strange light was seen near the spot; he became an object of veneration, and a chapel was put up to him, where the little tower is now.

7

Thurso, Reay, Halkirk and Watten

Thurso appears suddenly to the traveller who passes over Clardon Hill westwards. There it is, the largest town north of Inverness, sprawling up the valley of the Thurso river from the sea, white, clean-lined, almost Scandinavian. The meaning of the name is a subject of some dispute, but it is derived from the Norse for either 'bull-river' or 'Thor's river' and appears in the Icelandic sagas as *Pórsá*.

The town falls into three parts: the old area around the mouth of the river, the planned grid of streets that Sir John Sinclair laid out in the 1790s, and the modern estates on both sides of the river, all built since the 1950s. The old section clusters around the ruin of Old St Peter's kirk. Founded by Bishop Gilbert de Moravia in the thirteenth century, St Peter's remained the parish church of the town until 1832, when the new St Peter's was built in Sir John's Square. Most of the present building dates, however, from the seventeenth century and shows architectural features associated with the resurgence of Episcopacy during that century. Another feature, this time of hardline Presbyterianism, was the cutty stool where sinners found guilty by the Kirk Session were made to stand to suffer public humiliation; the cutty stool met an end, however, in about 1832 when, according to a local story, the friends of a young lad condemned to stand on it broke into the kirk and threw the offending piece of furniture into the river.

Old St Peter's suffered badly in a fire in the 1840s and remained a roofless ruin during a century of erosion and vandalism. The tracery window in the south gable was in imminent danger of collapse, but lack of funds and confusion over who was reponsible for the building prevented anything being done until quite recently. The Thurso Heritage Society was formed in 1981 and since has made the preservation of the old church a priority. The decay of the walls has been checked and work done on restoring and clearing up the structure, and it is hoped that before long the conservation programme will be completed to allow visitors access to this fine monument.

The lanes and streets around the church constituted the old town. Some of the buildings, notably in Shore Street, have been restored as dwelling houses and retain some of their early characteristics: the turnpike tower in Shore Street, for example, dates from 1696.

Thurso's trading history goes back many centuries. In 1330, when the Caithness parks were producing enough barley and oats to export, David II ordered that the weights and measures in use in the town should be the standard for the whole realm: 'Ane common and equal weicht, quhilk is called the weicht of Caithness (*pondus Cathaniae*) ... sall be keeped and used by all men within the realm of Scotland.' In 1633 the town became a free burgh of barony, and in a survey of Scottish ports made in 1656 it is listed as having two sloops of thirty tons. The records of the local Customs House, established in 1707, tell of an extensive trade, exporting meal, beef, hides, tallow and fish and importing timber, iron, wine, salt and coal. The present harbour was begun in 1891, but storm damage and a dispute between the building contractors and the Harbour Trustees caused such delay that the endeavour petered out before much of the work was completed. The failure to deepen the entrance kept out larger steamers and restricted vessels more or less to the smaller sailing schooners, which nevertheless came in great numbers for cargoes of flagstone from the works on the south side of the estuary. The harbour today is a quiet spot with only a fishing boat or two and a few pleasure craft to recall the past.

The shore to the east of the town is dominated by the woods and the ruined shell of Thurso East Castle, built in 1872 on the site of an older, seventeenth-century castle. It was here that Sir John Sinclair of Ulbster was born on 10 May 1754 – significantly the same year that saw the introduction of the potato to

Caithness. The ninth of eleven children, Sir John spent his boyhood in his native county before going south to study at Edinburgh. Although he spent a good deal of his adult life in London, he returned to Thurso every summer. Through his domination of the Age of Improvement, he acquired the nickname 'Agricultural Sir John'.

In the 1790s Sir John organized and edited the *Statistical Account of Scotland* and wrote the chapter on Thurso himself, intending it to be a model for his correspondents. His love of place shines through his prose. The air 'for about eight months of the year is ... pure and healthy', the scenery 'truly grand and picturesque', the people 'in general ... remarkably sober, regular, and attentive to business. Their favourite and indeed only public amusement is dancing, in which they are excellent proficients.' At the time, Thurso was a small town, with a population of about one thousand. There were two public and a number of private schools, the Customs House, a post office, a full range of tradespeople, a cart factory, a tannery, considerable shipping, a bank, two 'very good' inns, three surgeons, churches and 'pleasant villas'. However, the streets were unpaved and cluttered with middens. The first bridge over the river, built to Sir John's plan by Robert Tulloch, was opened in 1800; before that, one waded or used the coble ferry. The present bridge replaced its predecessor in 1887.

Sir John's creative energies were inexhaustible. He laid out a plan for the extension of the town, adopting a rectangular grid pattern with wide streets and spacious junctions. His layout forms the core of Thurso to this day, between the riverside Mall and Rose Street, and from Olrig Street south to Brabster Street. In the centre of the new development he set out a square, now named after him, with the road leading from it straight to the bridge. His effigy stands in the centre of the gardens. He wears the trews and plaid of the Fencible regiment that he founded and, of course, commanded during the Napoleonic wars. His view is interrupted today by the town's war memorial, and at the north-west side of the square are a monument and defunct drinking fountain erected to the memory of his son Sir George Sinclair of Ulbster. Sir John's Square also boasts the only permanent set of traffic lights in Caithness.

The old town and the new are connected by Rotterdam Street, carrying in its name a reminder of Thurso's trading days and now a pedestrian precinct. Among the interesting buildings in this part of the town are the Town Hall, opened in 1871 on the south side of the market square; the Tower Bar in the High Street, which has a round staircase extending onto the street, dates from about 1600. Miller Academy with its cupola dominates the end of Sinclair Street; the Academy, now the public library, began life in 1861 as the foremost school in the town. A conical, squat tower at the corner of Manson's Lane and Traill Street houses the Meadow Well, the town's major source of water until the beginning of this century. Manson's Lane also contains a fine old brewery building in the traditional, vernacular flagstone architecture.

Beside the Town Hall, in the old Carnegie Library, the Thurso Heritage Society intend to open a new museum to illustrate the history of the town and its hinterland. It has inherited the collections of the folk museum, formerly in this building, which include important Pictish stones and the plant collection of the Victorian botanist Robert Dick.

Dick lived at 8 Wilson Street from 1830 to 1866. A quiet, almost dour man, he arrived in Thurso at the age of nineteen to open a bakery, after his father, an exciseman who had already been posted to the town, had persuaded him to come. Dick worked as a baker until his death but his real interest lay far beyond ovens and dough. A lifelong bachelor, as soon as he had finished his daily baking he took to studying the natural world around him. He read voraciously and went for long, solitary walks in the countryside, returning late and often wet. He climbed Morven – a round walk of twenty-four hours from Thurso – at least four times. His reward was the friendship and respect of many of the scholars of this Victorian age of discovery; the townspeople thought him daft. He collected insects and plants, discovering species unrecorded before in the north, and studied the geology of the county to such effect that he overthrew many of the then current, but erroneous, theories about the northern environment. Sadly his reputation in his adopted town was almost non-existent, but after he died, on Christmas Eve 1866, a furore broke out in the local press as those who had previously ignored him rushed to defend their honour and claim that they had cared for him after all.

Thurso remained a fairly quiet place during the first part of this century. Then, in 1955, when operations began to develop the atomic energy establishment at Dounreay, the town experienced a sudden influx of people from England and southern Scotland; the population grew rapidly to almost ten thousand. New housing estates sprang up in a ring around the old town; a new high school, the first part of which was designed by Sir Basil Spence who also created the cathedral at Coventry, and a new technical college were built. Life changed irrevocably under this onslaught. Most of the incomers were welcomed, quickly settled down and were given the nickname 'atomics'. Their arrival led to the establishment of many new clubs and societies in the town and accounts for its present-day heterogenous character.

The harbour of Scrabster lies in the crook of an elbow of land to the west of Thurso. This is the terminus for the ferry to Orkney and, for a few years, a ferry to the Faroe Islands. Plans for an Iceland-Scrabster ferry are now being explored. Early in the nineteenth century a plan was put forward to make the bay here a base for the Royal Navy, but the Admiralty neglected the scheme until the First World War drew their attention to northern waters, and then they chose Scapa Flow in Orkney.

The road from Thurso to Scrabster passes the white farmhouse of Pennyland. Here in October 1854 was born Sir William Smith, the founder of the Boys' Brigade. Smith moved to Glasgow in his teens. He became a Sunday-school teacher, and it was a need to discipline Glaswegian bairns that, combined with his experiences in a volunteer regiment, gave him the idea of forming the first BB company in 1883.

In the twelfth century the bishops of Caithness kept a palace at Scrabster; almost all trace of it is gone now, but it was built by Gilbert de Moravia (who died in it in 1245) and probably stood close to the mouth of the burn that runs to the sea half-way between Thurso and the harbour. One of Bishop Gilbert's predecessors suffered cruelly at Scrabster, at the hands of Harald Maddadarson. After the defeat of Harald Ungi, William the Lion sent Rognvald Godrodarson, the Norse lord of the Hebrides, to invade Caithness. Harald prudently stayed in Orkney, leaving Rognvald to install stewards to govern the county, and then, after the Hebridean's departure, came over to re-establish his power. One of the stewards was killed and Harald himself had the Bishop of Caithness tortured at Scrabster. William the Lion was furious when he heard of this and led an army north of such a size that Harald chose to negotiate rather than fight. The parley took place probably at Ousdale on the Ord; in settlement, Harald promised to pay to the King one fourth of the land revenues of Caithness. Harald Maddadarson died in 1206, remembered as one of the most powerful earls to have held the north. The title passed to one of his sons, John, who was killed in a cellar in Thurso in 1231, the last of his line. The growing power of the Scots kings over Caithness was finally and formally recognized in 1266 when, in the Treaty of Perth, the county was ceded to Scotland.

The harbour at Scrabster is today a busy port: fishing boats come in to unload their catches and replenish their stores, there are numerous yachts and pleasure craft, and coasters call with oil and other cargoes. The lifeboat station was established in 1860, and in its first century saved over five hundred lives. Out beyond it is the lighthouse, also built in 1860, and from here a path leads to Holborn Head.

There is striking cliff scenery here: some glupes and the square, solid stack called the Clett. The view across the bay to Thurso and Dunnet Head and out to the ramparts of Hoy is very fine. An overgrown ditch cut across the point of the headland shows that this was a defended site in neolithic times. Modern defences are evidenced by the metallic sphere at West Murkle of an American naval base, part of a chain making up NATO's early warning system. (There is another base further west at Forss; Caithness and Sutherland may be at the end of Britain but their geographical position puts them in the front line of any war in the north Atlantic.)

The Orkney ferry began to operate from Scrabster in 1856, when John Stanger, a Stromness ship-builder, won the contract to carry the mail across the Firth. Stanger built his own ship, the *Royal Mail*, and sailed her to the Tyne to have her engines and paddlewheels fitted. She ran until 1869, when Stanger lost the contract, and was sold for conversion to a sailing vessel; only three months after her sale, she was wrecked in the Firth of Forth. The present ferry, owned by P & O, is called *Saint Ola*, and is the third ship on this route to bear the name.

In recent years Scrabster has become a popular centre for sea angling. Fishermen have been plucking gigantic fish from the sea here for centuries but it is only recently that records have been kept. Halibut over two hundred pounds are fairly common, and a conger eel weighing forty-five pounds was taken actually in Scrabster harbour. The European Sea-Angling Championships were held here in 1971, when 25,000 pounds of fish were caught, and they are due to take place at Scrabster again in 1985.

From Thurso the A882 runs south-east to Wick, cutting across the interior of Caithness. For the first five miles it follows the valley of the Thurso river, looking down on the railway line and the winding ribbon of water. The valley is broad and flat, and in winter the river spills over onto the fields in shining pools. The Thurso is a famous salmon water. Its length is divided into thirteen beats for anglers: in 1965 2,313 fish were taken in the season, but this figure is eclipsed by the record draught of salmon taken with a sweep net near the mouth of the river in 1736, when 2,560 were caught in one day. The conservation of salmon stocks is a pressing problem in the Highlands as a whole, as pollution and netting on the high seas have endangered the population. The fishing on the Thurso river is managed by Thurso Fisheries, who maintain a hatchery at Halkirk.

At Georgemas the road forks, the A895 branching off to the south to form the northern end of the Causewaymire. The A882 keeps its course onward through another gentle valley past Loch Scarmclate, more commonly known locally as Stemster Loch after the farm and hill on its north-west side, and towards Loch Watten.

Much of the interior of Caithness is fertile farmland. The fields are large and bordered with hedges, dry-stone dykes, fences and, in some places, slabs of flagstone set vertically in the ground – a mode of fencing unique to Caithness and another manifestation of the versatility of flagstone. Sometimes a thatched roof can be seen but most of the farm buildings are modern: tall silos rise from among the nineteenth-century steadings, and open-sided barns and sheds are common. Agriculture in Caithness and Sutherland is primarily concerned with livestock rearing, and the cultivation of cereals, mostly barley, and hay is largely directed towards providing winter feed for the animals. In recent years, farmers have introduced Continental breeds of cattle such as Charolais and Simmental to improve the quality of the native varieties. A few dairy farms provide milk for the local market, and butter and cheese are made. The formation of Caithness Livestock Breeders Ltd as a marketing co-operative in 1964 has done much to develop the north's reputation as a producer of quality meat, and it and other co-operatives are a major source for fertilizers, seeds and machinery.

Although the Age of Improvement brought eviction in its wake in Caithness as elsewhere, the number of people forced to quit the land was relatively low – individuals and families rather than whole communities, in most instances. At the same time the coastal villages were expanding and were able to absorb the shifting population, and, as Caithness was a region of arable as much as pastoral agriculture, the land was divided into enclosed farms rather than extensive sheep-runs. There was a crucial difference too in that nothing akin to the clan structure of Highland society really existed in 1800. Caithness was owned by forty-six or so lairds, half of them bearing the name Sinclair: the wealthiest were probably the Sinclairs of Ulbster, Sir John's family. In contrast, Sutherland, over three times the area of Caithness, had only twenty-six landowners, the largest by far being the earl's family.

Caithness tenants seem to have been more independently minded that their Sutherland counterparts and, although they were subservient to landlords, they do not appear to have entertained to any degree the ties of clan loyalty. The social structure was more that pertaining in lowland Scotland, perhaps a legacy of the Norse period with its more democratic spirit.

In the eighteenth century the Caithness lairds were a high-living lot. They imported luxurious foods – fruit, confectionery, the best teas, coffee and wines; they dressed in lace, linen and silk and subscribed to magazines and libraries. They also showed an extraordinary fondness for lawsuits, often, understandably, involving bankruptcy but equally as frequently concerned with disputes with their neighbours over land. Their wealth was dependent on the export of grain – oats and bere, a form of barley. The land and the sea were both fruitful. Several travellers commented on the cheapness of food and, although bad harvests happened here as elsewhere, the effects were generally less severe.

The tenants paid their rent in money and service. Sometimes remarkable amount of time and goods accrued to the lairds. The laird of Weydale and Todholes received in 1762 from eighteen tenants 109 bolls of meal, 90 fowls, peats to the value of £80, 21 geese, over £277 in cash, and unlimited labour for cutting peats and for farmwork. During the Age of Improvement such income was converted to straight cash payments of rent.

The standard of living of the ordinary people was low. Before 1790 there were no carts in Caithness: packhorses carried loads over long distances, but around the farms it was the women who bore the heaviest burdens. Thomas Pennant observed with horror in 1769 how they traipsed with groaning baskets of peat, dung or seaweed, which the men filled. Their homes were often simple stone and turf huts, with livestock and humans using the same entrance. In 1829 one traveller said the houses and the peatstacks were 'one scarcely distinguishable from the other, for the cottages are built of turf and stone, and when thatched are secured by cords of twisted heather thrown across the roof'.

With the formation of enclosed, moderately sized farms, those who would have been tenants of small plots became either crofters or farm labourers. On the larger farms there grew up the society of the ploughmen who, under the command of the farmer or his foreman, the grieve, worked the horses that provided the energy for the farming revolution. The big farms had a heavy demand for labour; with their numbers of farm servants they became almost small villages in their own right. Married men and women lived in cottages which came with the job, and when they moved from one farm to another, they moved house as well. Unmarried men lived in bothies, and their way of life attracted much criticism from the ministers: 'Deeds of shame are shamelessly committed in those dens of darkness,' wrote the Reverend Charles Thomson of Wick. 'The light of day cannot be let in on a Caithness bothy.' This is an exaggeration. But it is true that the farm servants worked hard and played hard in their scant leisure hours, and probably drank more than was good for them.

Ploughs are no longer dragged across the parks by pairs of Clydesdale horses, but the ploughing still marks the beginning of the farm year. Some farmers like to start ploughing as soon as the previous year's grain has been won from the field, but others prefer to wait until spring before they draw the iron coulters through the dun stubble. Sowing and planting are nearly always done now by tractors drawing appropriate implements behind them, but older techniques such as the sowing of corn by hand persisted on smaller crofts until the 1960s. There are two main harvests, with a smaller ingathering later in the autumn when the potatoes are ready for lifting. The hay harvest takes place first, in summer: hay is cut, allowed to dry for a while and then baled for winter fodder. In September combine harvesters attack the barley and oats; the grain is dried and stored, and the straw, if it is not burned, is kept to bed the cattle when they are indoors during the winter.

The breeding of cattle and sheep is arranged so that calving and lambing take place in the spring. Calves are usually born indoors from January through to April, though sometimes later. Lambs see their first daylight in less comfortable surroundings, in the lee of a dyke or a whin bush, though some ewes are brought inside before birth, if time allows. These are anxious days for the farmer, for his year's income depends more or less on the successful birth and upbringing of his animals.

In the summer months the various agricultural shows are held. Farmers and their families gather to show off their best animals and have a day out; salesmen compete to display the latest in agricultural machinery; contractors offer to carry out ditching, drainage and other tasks; and sideshows and vendors plunge raucously into separating the public from their cash. Various competitions – show-jumping, tug o'war, carriage driving – enliven the occasion and sometimes bring back a whiff of the older days of the 'farmtouns'.

Loch Watten lies roughly in the centre of lowland Caithness. This three-mile stretch of water is noted for the quality of its trout, and in winter large flocks of geese and ducks dot its surface. The countryside around it is, for Caithness, relatively well wooded: hedges divide the fields and line the roads, and small plantations defy the gales around the larger farm steadings.

Watten is simply the Norse word for water – *vatn* – and is also the name of the village at the south end of the loch. With its kirks, its school and its post office, it forms the centre for the parish. Its minister commented in the 1790s that 'its inhabitants are all employed in the business of farming', and this is true still to a considerable extent today. It seems highly appropriate that Watten should have been the birthplace of the Scottish Young

Farmer movement; the first club was formed here in 1923. Watten was also the birthplace in 1810 of Alexander Bain, who invented, among other things, the first electric clock. A monument to his memory stands in the village.

In the late 1970s a series of excavations were made at Clow, about two miles south of Watten beside the Acharole burn, on the site of an ancient chapel. The site is close to Scouthal, where a mill was recorded in 1527 and indicates that this area may have been of some importance before the present village of Watten grew up in the last two centuries. Chapel-building at Clow seems to have occurred in two phases; although there is a lack of evidence, it is possible that the site was a sacred place in the early Christian period before the twelfth century. Human remains have been found in the vicinity, including some mysterious burials of skulls; Clow may have been the original parish church.

Several roads lead away from Watten: the A882 continues to Wick; a road runs up the valley of the Strath burn, the headwaters of the Wick river, to Camster; the B870 passes by the end of Loch Watten in a series of tight curves and ascends to the higher ground on the north. I wish, however, to take the traveller along the B870 westwards from Watten to Mybster and the Dales.

Mybster is a crossroads. There used to be an inn here, marking the end of the dreary crossing of the Causewaymire for Thurso-bound travellers. Just to the north of the junction rises Spittal Hill, its flattened, conical shape a landmark in this part of the county; its name reveals that a hospital, a refuge for travellers, once existed in its vicinity.

John Sinclair of Scotscalder raised a banner on Spittal Hill in 1746 in support of the Jacobites, but only forty-three men turned out, although they all had good horses and weapons. Sinclair's contingent was present at the débâcle at Little Ferry when Cromarty's men were routed; Sinclair himself escaped in a boat, losing only his hat to the bullets whirring around him.

The flagstone quarries at Achanarras on the side of Spittal Hill are one of the best sites for fossil fishes in Caithness, so much so that in recent years amateur collectors, European as well as British, have caused damage in their search for specimens. The Nature Conservancy Council (its local headquarters is at

Golspie) finally stepped in and concluded an access agreement with the owners of the quarries, restricting fossil-hunting to those with proper permits. In 1981 the quarries were purchased by the Council and declared a National Nature Reserve.

The rocks underlying most of Caithness belong to the grouping known as Old Red Sandstone, laid down during the Devonian era between 400 and 350 million years ago, when a great shallow lake called by geologists Orcadie covered what is now the northern extremities of Scotland as far as Shetland. This was the time of the evolution of the fishes, and many specimens of species now extinct were preserved in the accumulating sediments that time transformed into Caithness flagstone. Jack Saxon's little book *The Fossil Fishes of Caithness* makes a splendid introduction to the subject.

The B870 continues west from Mybster to Westerdale, where there are some fine buildings, including a mill and the doocot at Dale House, in traditional flagstone architecture. Here we are once again in the valley of the Thurso river, and a minor road runs from Westerdale up through empty moorland to Strathmore Lodge and beyond to Loch More. To the east of Loch More lies Blar nam Faoileag, 'the bog of the seagull', an area of over eleven thousand acres of wetland of recognized international ecological importance as an undisturbed bog habitat.

Two miles to the south of Westerdale are the ruins of Dirlot Castle. David Miller, an authority on the castles of Caithness, has described Dirlot as occupying 'the most picturesque position' of any of the numerous fortified sites in the county. It is very striking, a keep on top of a craggy pinnacle rising in the centre of a gorge cut into the moors by the river; the gorge and its cliffs, maybe fifty feet high, are a surprise, hidden until the last moment from anyone approaching from a distance. Only a few courses of the stone work of the keep remain, but the walls were over six feet thick and, in medieval times, impregnable. Close to the castle is a small graveyard with, among more recent graves, several eighteenth-century tombstones. One reads:

THIS STONE IS BROU
GHT HERE BY DONALD
GUNN IN CARNMUCK
WHO WAS IN HIS MA

JESTIES SERVICE TO
THE MEMORY OF DO
GUNN HIS FATHER
WHO DYED JAN 9
1726 ...

Dirlot is believed to have been a seat of Reginald de Cheyne, who was of Norman descent and held extensive tracts of Caithness in the thirteenth and fourteenth centuries. De Cheyne's signature appears on Scotland's Declaration of Independence at Arbroath in 1320, so perhaps he fought for Robert Bruce. The *Statistical Account of Scotland* describes a fortified hunting lodge of de Cheyne's at Loch More but no trace of this building is left.

The last de Cheyne died in 1350. He had no sons, and his properties passed through the marriage of his two daughters into other families: Marjory married in 1337 the second son of the Earl of Sutherland, and Mary became wife to John Keith of the Ackergill family.

Some time after this, a feud developed between the Keiths and the Gunns. It began with a certain Dugald Keith's jealousy of Helen Gunn. When this girl, reputedly of matchless beauty, was about to be married, Dugald and some cronies kidnapped her and bore her off to Ackergill where, in James Calder's words, she 'became the victim of the brutal and licentious Keith'. Despair drove Helen to throw herself from the top of Ackergill Tower, and no Gunn could live on amicable terms with a Keith after that.

The Gunns, themselves no exemplars of virtue and good citizenship, were already at odds with the Mackays of Strathnaver, whom they raided frequently, carrying off cattle and gear. In 1426 the two clans fought an indecisive battle at Harpsdale south of Halkirk. The Keiths formed an alliance with the Mackays and fought their mutual enemy in 1438 at Tannach Moor, south-west of Wick; the Gunns were defeated with much slaughter.

The leader of the Gunns at this time was Crowner George, *Am Braisdeach Mor*, whom we have already met at his castle at Halberry Head. In 1464 Dirlot also belonged to him. George felt a need to settle the feud with the Keiths, and the two families agreed each to send twelve horsemen to a conference; if a peaceful settlement proved impossible, armed conflict between the two 'teams' would be resorted to. There are different versions of what happened: the confrontation took place in either 1464 or 1478, and either in Strathmore or at the chapel of St Tears between Noss Head and Ackergill. (The latter site seems more likely, although it is very close to the Keiths' castle. There is no trace of a chapel there now, but it was dedicated to the tears of the mothers of Bethlehem weeping for their first-born slaughtered by Herod.) The twelve Gunns arrived first and went into the chapel to pray. While they were on their knees, the Keiths rode up – with two men on each horse – and promptly attacked. The Gunns fought tenaciously but in the end they were all overwhelmed. George the Crowner and some of his sons fell, but his eldest son, James, had not been in the chosen dozen and survived. He went to live in the Strath of Kildonan where, many years later, his son finally avenged the treachery by ambushing the Keiths and massacring them while they were travelling through the hills.

By following the B870 from Westerdale to Thurso, we pass the former power station at Braehour where in the 1950s experiments were made on using peat to generate electricity.

The detailed story of attempts to exploit peat is told by Jim Johnston in his book *A Future for Peat*. The fact that Caithness and Sutherland have about forty per cent of their land area under peat has led to the proposal of many schemes for its large-scale use. Legend tells that it was a Norseman, Torf Einar, who taught how peat should be cut: we can safely ignore this litle conceit on the part of the saga-writers and accept that peat was in use as a source of fuel centuries before the longships crunched ashore in Caithness.

Travellers can see easily the trenches where peat is cut, scarring the moors of the county. It is a traditional pursuit that has changed little over the years. A family can rent or obtain the right to cut peat and, although it is hard work, it is not unpleasant – a summer job, and often a social one. The dialect has a number of words to describe the various stages in the preparation of dry fuel from the sodden peat. Using a spade, the cutter first cleans the 'bank' to allow better drainage. A 'flachter spade', with a wide blade, is then used to 'turr' the bank – that is, to remove the layer of heather and turf growing on the surface. After this, the 'tuskar', a spade with a very sharp blade and a lug

The coast at Drumbeg.

Quinag emerging from the mist.

Suilven, its sugarloaf peaks shrouded in cloud.

at right angles to the main blade, is used to slice the soft peat and lift it from the ground. Some cutters do their own 'lifting' but usually a helper 'lifts' the cut slab and passes it to the 'scaler', who spreads the slabs out to dry in the sun and wind. It takes only a few days for a skilled team to cut a year's supply for the household. As the peat dries, its consistency changes from being a soggy, soft slab to a hard, biscuit-like brick. In this form it undergoes only very slow degradation and easily lasts a year or more. To speed the drying process, the slabs are set up in herring-bone rows or stacked in open piles; when a few weeks have passed, they are brought home usually by tractor to be built into a peatstack close to the house. The building of the peatstack is itself a skilled task; the correct laying of the walls will keep the peats on the inside dry. The 'hill' as the moors are called, enabled even the poorest cottar at least to keep warm.

Peat formation has been an almost continual process since the end of the Ice Ages, though the rate of formation has varied according to fluctuations in climate. The bogs of Strath Halladale and Altnabreac, those which would have fed the Braehour power station, average about seven feet in depth. The Republic of Ireland and the Soviet Union make extensive use of their peat deposits, and the experience especially of the former inspired the trials at Braehour.

The Scottish Peat Committee was set up by the government in 1949 and, with the North of Scotland Hydro-Electric Board, backed the experiment. Special turbines were built at Clydebank and were installed at Braehour. Trials began in 1959 but technical difficulties delayed progress, until the scheme was abandoned and the machinery sold in 1962. For a time, however, peat-generated electricity was fed into the National Grid, and some of it was used, ironically, in the construction of the atomic power station at Dounreay.

When the Braehour scheme started, it was a topic of much interest. The late Donald Grant, the rector of Thurso High School and one of the best dialect poets, summed up the expectancy and humour of the situation in a poem called 'Peats for Power'. Here is one verse, the thoughts of a crofter on the benefits he may presently enjoy:

So God-speed till e flachter spade

An God-speed till e tuskar!
A'll hev a 'lectric razor then
Till shift ma bit o whuskar.
A'm thinkan too till keep a coo
We 'lectric licht abeen 'er,
An e'en for muckan oot e byre
A'll hev a vac'um cleaner!

The power station at Braehour is now empty, but the peat is still there, growing thicker, and the day may come when this new industry manages a successful second start. As things stand, peat is cut by machine along the Causewaymire, and experiments have been made at Halkirk in using a peat-fired heating system in the primary school.

At Scotscalder the B870 rises to pass over the railway line. Slightly to the north is Loch Calder, the main water-supply for most of the county. The districts of Calder and Scotscalder mark another part of the boundary zone between Norse and Gaelic cultures: Calder is derived most probably from Kalfadalr, 'the valley of the calf', whereas Scotscalder indicates the place where the Scots, that is Gaelic-speakers, lived.

To the west of Scotscalder Beinn Freiceadain, the watchtower mountain, and Ben Dorrery rise in a prominent ridge. Neither hill is of exceptional height – Ben Dorrery, the higher, is just over eight hundred feet – but, relative to the sweep of the Caithness moors, both are very prominent. It is not surprising to find the remains of a neolithic fort on the summit of Beinn Freiceadain, and there are many cairns and standing stones in the district.

The railway line connects Scotscalder with what is probably the most lonely settlement in Caithness – Altnabreac. A handful of houses, the station and a school (with four pupils at the time of writing) make up the village. Train passengers will see also the isolated, baronial grandeur of the Lochdhu Hotel, a fishing hotel a mile south-east of Altnabreac. An immense stretch of moor, threaded by burns and glimmering with lochans, runs along the border between Caithness and Sutherland from Morven north almost to Reay. The train takes one through it, but for a closer look it is necessary to walk.

Two miles to the north of Scotscalder a minor road leads one east to Halkirk. This is the largest village in the interior of the county, its street laid out in a spacious grid, the design another product of Sir John Sinclair's relentless improving in 1803. The name of the village is Norse – Ha-kirkja, 'high church' – and reflects the fact that the bishops of Caithness once had a palace here. The ecclesiastical history of the place, however, goes back further to Pictish times. The Skinnet stone, an oblong slab with two beautifully carved crosses and some Pictish symbols, used to stand here on the site of a chapel dedicated to St Thomas; it is now part of the Thurso Heritage collection and will be displayed in the new museum.

The most famous bishop to have his residence here is undoubtedly Adam, who was consecrated in 1214. In 1220 the people of the district, enraged by the bishop's increases in taxation, particularly over the amounts of butter to be paid to the church, broke into the palace. A monk was killed, and Adam was seized and, in the words of a letter written by the Pope in 1222, was 'stripped' of his clothing, 'stoned', 'mortally wounded ... with an axe' and 'burned ... in his own kitchen'. (On his elevation to the bishopric in 1223, Gilbert de Moravia chose to reside at Dornoch; perhaps Adam's fate was a factor in his decision.) The dissident parishioners at Halkirk suffered severely for their crime, and this grim incident has remained part of our folkloric history when much else has been forgotten.

The Thurso river is broad and swift where it passes through Halkirk. Sir John Sinclair's grandfather was the first to conceive of a bridge here, and he left money in his will for its construction. It was not completed until 1731, some years after his death, but it lasted until 1970, when it was pulled down and replaced. The streets of the village bear the names of members of the Sinclair family. Two of the wells that were sunk to serve the community still exist in Bridge Street. The imposing building with the mock baronial tower overlooking the bridge is the Ross Institute, which was founded by John Ross who emigrated from Gerston to New Zealand in 1861 and did well enough to be able to endow this community centre in his native village. When the Institute opened in 1911, its electric clock was the first to appear in a public building in Scotland.

In a clump of woodland on the north bank of the Thurso one can find the broken tower of Braal Castle. The square, ruined keep dates from the Norse period and is the best preserved of the more ancient fortresses of Caithness. Harald Maddadarson's son,

John, lived here, and through the centuries it passed into and out of the possession of the different families that held the earldom of the county, ending up with the Sinclairs of Ulbster.

To the east of Halkirk is Georgemas Junction, where the railway lines from Wick and Thurso join to make the single track running south to Sutherland and ultimately to Inverness. The small station here comes alive when the trains arrive and have to be split or linked together. The place is named for a fair that used to be held here on St George's day.

From Halkirk the B874 runs north to Thurso along the west side of the river valley. On the way it passes Skinnet, named from the Norse *skinandi*, meaning 'the shining one' and a reference to the river, and once the site of a parish church. The parish of Skinnet was united with that of Halkirk in the sixteenth century.

As the road nears Thurso, it is joined by the B870; only a short distance beyond this junction a minor road runs off to the west to the small village of Westfield on the east bank of the River Forss. The upper reaches of the Forss flow through the district of Broubster, now almost empty of people but until the beginning of this century home to a community of crofters and one of the last areas in Caithness to have Gaelic as a day-to-day language.

A road follows the course of the Forss north to join the A836 at Bridge of Forss and bring us back to the main coast road along the north of Scotland. Brims Ness protrudes in a blunt headland: the sea thrashing on the rocks at its point gives the place its Norse name from *brim*, 'surf'. The keep of Brims Castle, a former Sinclair stronghold, forms part of the buildings of the farm, the Mains of Brims, and on the headland can be found the ruins of an old chapel.

About a mile to the west, where the Forss enters the sea through a litle sandy bay, is the district of Crosskirk and the remains of what is probably the oldest chapel in the county. St Mary's was built in the twelfth century; only its walls stand today, windowless and thick. The chapel has both nave and chancel, the two chambers connected by a low door with a large lintel stone and inclined jambs, features it shares with other chapels in Shetland and Orkney and with some early oratories in Ireland. Surrounded by gravestones, the little chapel is sturdy and carries an air of peace in its simplicity.

Bridge of Forss is a picturesque spot. The river drops over a series of cataracts past the large, old mill frames against the plantations of trees around Forss House.

West of Forss three miles, one passes Dounreay. The sprawling establishment, built on an abandoned Second World War airfield, is easily recognized by the distinctive sphere that housed the first experimental reactor. One writer referred to it as a giant golf ball waiting to be teed off into the north Atlantic. The 'dome', to give it its familiar Caithness name, stands as an odd perfect shape among the curves and irregular angles of rock and field.

Dounreay is the biggest single employer in Caithness, and its presence for the last thirty-odd years has made the people of the county more open-minded about the nuclear power industry than probably any other community in Britain. Indeed, there is an active group campaigning to bring more of the nuclear industry to the county. There is an exhibition on the site where visitors can learn something of the work done here.

The construction of the Dounreay site began in 1955, and almost simultaneously Thurso girded itself to meet an influx of people such as it had never experienced before. There were some doubts expressed about the safety of this new industry but in general the mood was one of excited anticipation, fuelled by the deeply felt sense that until then the economy of the north had been sinking out of control. Dounreay meant jobs and security – and still does. As a small boy at the time, I took a perverse pride in the belief that, if Dounreay blew up, 'Caithness would disappear from the map.' Government documents recently made public under the thirty-year rule show that Westminster too was concerned with the risks of explosion. Dounreay was chosen because it was 'far enough from a town'; Harlech in Wales and Golspie had been considered too densely populated to permit any evacuation.

Since then Dounreay has become an accepted part of local life. Any rumour that the plant is to close makes instant headlines. There was little protest in Caithness when it was announced that Altnabreac was to be the first site to be tested for the possible storage of nuclear waste underground, in contrast to Orkney where plans to develop uranium mining were rejected outright, and Scourie where the local people rose against test-drilling similar to that at Altnabreac. Later studies suggested that coastal sites, such as the pre-Cambrian rocks in the Cape Wrath area, might be better for waste disposal. The test-drilling at Altnabreac was abandoned in 1980, and in 1981 the government announced that any decision on the underground storage of nuclear waste was to be put back for fifty years.

The fast reactor at Dounreay became the first of its kind in the world to produce electricity for public use; in October 1962 it pumped two megawatts into the National Grid. The first reactor's successor produces electricity in much larger quantities; in 1983–4 135 megawatts were bought by the Hydro Board, and it intends to build up generation capacity to 250 megawatts.

Activities at Dounreay have come in for a good deal of criticism in recent years. It has been alleged that plutonium has gone missing from the plant, that accidents have been hushed up and that workers have been exposed to dangerous levels of radiation. There has also been angry concern over plans to ship plutonium nitrate, a byproduct of fast reactor operations, through the stormy waters of the Minch and the Pentland Firth. The Atomic Energy Authority has worked hard to fend off these attacks, claiming that the issues and incidents have been alarmingly exaggerated and conclusions drawn without sufficient knowledge on the part of the critics.

Two miles west of Dounreay is Sandside Bay, a lovely inlet of sand with a small harbour built by James Bremner in about 1830 on the west side. Three burns drain into the bay, cutting shallow courses across the sand. The place was attractive to the earliest settlers in the north, too, it seems, for archaeologists have identified the marks of prehistoric human activity at Cnoc Stanger beside the Sandside Burn.

The village of Reay extends along the main road just inland from the bay. The name of the village is probably derived from the Norse *ra*, a corner, although a possible alternative source is *rath*, Gaelic for fort. The remains of the old kirk stand in one corner of the present churchyard; the white kirk was built in 1739 and has in its south wall iron loops, the 'jougs' where minor criminals were chained up for public opprobrium. The medieval village stood closer to the sea than its successor, but its market cross, a worn, hammer-headed pillar, was moved to grace the roadside in the new village. Two fairs used to be held here, at Marymas in August and at Kenlamas in December.

One of the famous ministers to occupy the church here was Alexander Pope. Two years before he was ordained at Reay, he had gone to London to meet his namesake, the author of *The Rape of the Lock*, who, it is said, received him well and gave him books and an ornamental snuffbox. Pope was in the habit of belabouring backward parishioners with a cudgel to drive them to the kirk. He also translated Torfaeus' *Ancient History of Orkney, Caithness and the North*, studied Gaelic and antiquities, married twice and fathered eight children. In his last years before his death in 1782, he suffered paralysis and had to be carried to the pulpit to lead worship.

Sandside House, in its woods on the west side of the village, was the laird's home. The estate included the lands of Broubster, Shebster and Shurrery in the valley of the Forss, and it was from here that probably the largest evictions in Caithness took place in the 1830s: according to Donald Mackay in *This Was My Glen*, 192 families were removed. Some settled in Reay itself, others left the district entirely, and some built and lived in the block of houses at Broubster known as 'The Square'.

Reay was the birthplace and home of one of Caithness's most famous rhymers. Henry Henderson was born in a croft in 1873; he published his first poem in the *John O'Groat Journal* in 1892, and until his death in 1957, continued to produce verse at a terrific rate – sentimental, humorous and nostalgic poems about the events and places around him. Known as 'the Bard o'Reay', he wrote verses that were copied and kept by many admirers.

To the west of Reay the A836 begins to rise over moorland. The countryside becomes more rugged, grass gives way to heather: we are leaving Caithness and are about to enter Sutherland once more. Like the Ord, the border is desolate and bare, appearing more so without the steep braes that characterize the other frontier. The boundary between the two Districts is, of course, signposted, but nearby there is a more remarkable waymark: an enormous boulder cleaved through the middle as if by an axe. The Devil caused the split when, according to one of several stories connected with the spot, he left Melvich in high dudgeon at the people's incorruptability and headed for Caithness where the folk were more welcoming. As he crossed the border, he took a swipe at the stone with his tail to relieve his frustration and

8

From Melvich to Cape Wrath

The road along the north coast of Sutherland runs from one strath to another across intervening stretches of moor, dipping past beautiful beaches and offering eye-filling views of hills, cliffs and sea. The first strath just to the west of the Caithness border is that of the River Halladale, through which the A897 passes to Helmsdale on the east coast.

The Halladale rises in the moors to the north of Knockfin and collects water from many burns on its journey. One of these drains the land around Forsinard, almost on the watershed between the Halladale system and the flood basin of the Helmsdale river. Here, too, the railway line to Caithness turns east after its threading of the Strath of Kildonan and clambers up to the county march. In winter trains have been caught here by drifting snow, giving rise to the unkind though not entirely undeserved nickname for Forsinard of 'frozen hard'. The most recent entrapment occurred in January 1984, when the occupants of the train had to be rescued by helicopter.

The first settlement along the north coast that the traveller reaches is Melvich, strung out along the A836 on the western side of the Halladale estuary. The beach at the mouth of the river shows how it got its name – from the Gaelic for sand dunes. On the east side of the river is Bighouse, a seat of the Mackays in the past. From Melvich a loop of road runs out through the village of Portskerra, which has a small harbour tucked into a cove close to the point of the headland Rubha Bhra. This area also marks the boundary between the sandstone rocks to the east and the unyielding granite underlying the land further west.

The change in the landscape is very noticeable on the way from Melvich to Strathy. Moors come right to the edge of the road which twists and rises and falls on its way across them; there are no longer the long stretches of straight asphalt that characterize driving in Caithness.

A few miles to the west of Melvich another river and another bay punctuate the land, at Strathy. A minor road provides a route up the valley of the Strathy as far as the high moors to the west of the Griam hills; this area is largely empty of human habitation, in contrast to the crofting district around Strathy Bay. A bridge like a giant coat-hanger carries the main road across the river. Strathy Point, reaching north like a long finger into the sea, is tipped by an automatic lighthouse.

The pattern of strath, crofts and river is repeated at Armadale, three miles to the west, and again at Kirtomy, before we reach the large, scattered village of Bettyhill. The villages in this area date from the 1790s, when tenants were settled along the coast to make room for sheep-walks in the interior. The intention of the landlords was that the tenants should turn to the sea for their livelihood, and to encourage them to exchange their spades for boats the amount of land allotted to each household was as little as two acres.

Bettyhill and its neighbouring settlement of Farr form the centre of the parish of Farr, which gets its name from the Gaelic *faire*, a lookout or watch, taken to refer to the time in the Dark Ages when sentinels on the northern shore kept their eyes open for signs of approaching Vikings. A chain of duns, with attendant watchfires, stretching inland up Strathnaver for over twenty-four miles, can be traced, lending support to this concept.

The old parish church at Farr has been converted into a museum of local history and has a large number of exhibits of articles and bric-à-brac from different periods. There is also here a Mackay Room, a focus for the Clan Mackay Society, one of the oldest of the modern clan associations. One feature of the museum is that the local schoolchildren are involved in the presentation of the subject matter, and their paintings and graphics adorn the walls. The church itself dates from 1774, but in the graveyard at the west end is an intriguing relic of the earliest days of Christianity in the area. The Farr Stone is an upright pillar bearing a cross and Celtic designs as well as Pictish symbols. Off the coast, three miles to the west, is a small island known as Eilean Neave, 'holy island', and the whole district is rich in legends and more tangible monuments of the itinerant missionaries who brought the gospel here.

The pupils of the secondary school at Farr have twice taken their own musical shows to the Edinburgh Festival. The first one, *Run Rig*, in 1979, expressed their concern for the future of their community, their special place, and took a wry look at the contemporary state of the north. One song had the words: 'We had Norman lairds, Scottish lairds, English lairds and Texan lairds, and Dutch and Japanese lairds ... to see the Highlands alive again needs a different point of view.' Memories of the Clearances and the issue of land-use and ownership are very much alive here.

The River Naver flows past the hill on which Bettyhill stands and discharges into the bay of Torrisdale. The broad curve of the beach extends from the Naver to the Borgie river, a mile of sand that forms part of the Invernaver National Nature Reserve. The latter was created in 1960 and has a total area of 1,363 acres, protecting an assemblage of plants unique in the north. Here montane and oceanic species mingle, the mildness customarily associated with low altitude being offset by the effects of latitude to permit plants more at home in high, exposed conditions to flourish at sea-level. The wind-blown sand also tempers the acidity of the moors to produce a calcareous soil. Among the saxifrages and other alpine species, one can find the very rare *Primula scotica*, a primrose with delicate purple petals that has become something of a symbol of the north.

Strathnaver runs inland from Bettyhill for over twenty miles. The B873 follows the west bank of the river, and a minor road runs for a short distance down the east bank as far as Skelpick, where there is a long cairn similar to the one at Camster. The strath shows many signs of having been a major centre of population in the neolithic era and Bronze Age: two men erecting a fence at Chealamy in 1980 uncovered a Bronze Age cist containing a large earthenware beaker and decorated with geometrical designs.

Much of the Strath is wooded now with conifers, but in the recent past it was more open. The valley was home to several small communities of twenty or so families who tilled the land in run-rig fashion, sharing the use of draught animals. Life was not idyllic but it was easier than in such parts of the county as the north-west coast. A survey in 1811 ascribed to each household in Strathnaver twelve cattle, six horses, fifteen to twenty sheep, goats and two acres of arable land. Also, men from the area were serving in the army, and they, and men such as Donald Macleod, who travelled widely to ply his trade of stonemason, must have remitted sums of cash to their relatives at home. In 1803 and again in 1807–8 there was dearth after bad harvests, and some families had already emigrated voluntarily to North American by this time.

In 1792–4 Clearances took place in the north, and people were resettled at Armadale and Portskerra, but it was not until the arrival of Patrick Sellar and William Young in 1809 that Strathnaver was cleared. Both men came from Morayshire, where the new methods of agriculture had already been adopted. Sellar has become something of a bogey man, the villain of the Clearances; the reputation is not undeserved. A portrait in the Farr Museum shows him and his wife to have the appearance of a fairly ordinary farming couple of the period; a Gaelic poet, however, described him as having a 'nose ... like an iron plough-blade ... and hindquarters like an ass'. He was about thirty when in 1809 he became the Duke of Sutherland's factor in Strathnaver. His fellow-countryman, Young, was appointed estate commissioner, and together they implemented the policies of land clearance in the parishes of Dornoch, Rogart, Loth, Clyne, Golspie and Assynt. In 1813 they turned their attention to Strathnaver.

In December of that year, some two dozen tenants from the strath were summoned to Golspie, where, at an inn, they were given a lecture by Young about the forthcoming evictions. Their minister, David Mackenzie, translated the Commissioner's words into Gaelic and at the same time bade his parishioners obey those placed in authority over them. Sellar himself wanted to lease Strathnaver to add to the estates he already held at Morvich on the east coast, and he lost no time issuing the tenants with notices to quit. Plots of land were to be made ready for them to occupy by Whitsun 1814, the deadline for removal. But there were delays in the surveying and allocation of the coastal land, and the plots were not ready until June, which left the tenants only ten days in which to pack up and flit. Sellar's impatience got the better of him, and on 13 June he began evicting the tenants. The inhabitants of each house were thrown out with their property, and their homes were burnt. A bed-ridden woman in her nineties was dragged from one house in the nick of time. In all, twenty-seven families were evicted in the first week, and others later.

'Many deaths ensued from alarm, fatigue and cold,' wrote Donald Macleod, of whom more below. 'Some old men took to the woods and precipices, wandering about in a state approaching to, or of absolute insanity.... Pregnant women were taken with premature labour, and several children died.' Macleod may have exaggerated the number of deaths, but the events were horrible enough. The people gathered their possessions and their wits as best they could, and moved to the coast. 'They suffered very much for the want of houses,' recalled one man. For shelter, they built walls of sod and stretched blankets across the top, and in such hovels they spent the following winter before they could build proper homes.

In 1816 Patrick Sellar was brought to trial in Inverness on charges of oppression, arson and causing the deaths of two old people in Strathnaver. The jury, predominantly landowners, found him not guilty. He lost his position as factor with the Duke but remained in possession of his sheep-farm in Strathnaver, where he evicted his remaining tenants in 1819, though taking care not to deal too harshly with them. On this occasion some of the people accepted small farms in Caithness, but most settled on the north coast. Among those who went at this time was Robert Gordon, the tacksman of Strathnaver, an old man living at Langdale and, until the arrival of Sellar, the immediate landlord of the tenants. Ironically, Gordon was a descendant of the old Gordon earls of Sutherland and had been Sellar's host when the factor had first come to the strath. In the new order, there was no room for tacksmen.

On 19 September 1981 Dr Ian Grimble unveiled a monument to Donald Macleod at the Red Brae in upper Strathnaver. A stonemason and an eyewitness of the Clearances, Macleod was born at the nearby village of Rossal; evicted, he moved with his family to Bettyhill. Outraged and angry at the cruelty with which his people had been thrown off the land, he began to speak out against the evictions. In 1818 he married a girl from Farr and eventually settled at Strathy Point, looking after not only his own children but many of his in-laws. His outspoken condemnation of the Clearances made him a target, and in 1827 he was accused and found guilty of being in debt. Macleod maintained that the charges against him were false and appealed to the Duke and Duchess of Sutherland. They granted him permission to remain on their estates pending further inquiry. The latter was held by James Loch, one of the Duke's ablest administrators, who found Macleod guilty of the charges. The local minister, probably under pressure from the factors, had refused to sign a certificate stating Macleod to be an 'honest and peaceful character'. Although the minister later signed the certificate, when forced to by several witnesses, the authorities had the wherewithal to act. On 20 October 1830, while Macleod was away, his wife, five children and furniture were thrown out of their home. The house was boarded up to prevent re-entry, and neighbours were warned not to shelter the family lest they sought eviction themselves. Leaving her children, Mrs Macleod set off to walk through chilly, wet weather to Caithness; at Sandside she was given shelter by the laird, William Innes, who offered her the use of a house he owned at Armadale. Meanwhile, Macleod had sensed that something was wrong and had set out homewards from Wick. He caught up with his wife as she was trudging towards Armadale and found his fears realized. Back at Strathy, they found the children had been given shelter for the night at a relative's house.

At Armadale Macleod continued to suffer harassment from the factors, and in 1831 he brought his family to Edinburgh, where he began writing to the newspapers about the evictions. His articles and pamphlets were collected and published as one volume in 1856: the title *Gloomy Memories* was a deliberate rebuttal of the book *Sunny Memories* in which Harriet Beecher Stowe, the author of *Uncle Tom's Cabin*, had ecstatically praised the improvement work of the Duke of Sutherland. By the time his book appeared, Donald Macleod had emigrated with his family to Ontario, where he later died.

The site of the village of Rossal, Macleod's birthplace, can be reached by following a forestry road along the east bank of the

Naver from the road junction at Syre. The last mile from the car-park to the village has to be walked. Signposts and explanatory plaques guide the visitor around the ruins. It is a melancholy spot, the air heavy with the resinous scent of the conifer plantations that enclose the site. When the trees were planted in 1961, the Forestry Commission left the ruins of Rossal bare. Thirteen families once lived here, tilling forty-six acres of arable ground and keeping animals on thirty-four acres of rough pasture. It takes about twenty minutes for a fit person to walk around Rossal and see the stumps of the old houses, but it is a walk that every landowner in the Highlands should be made to take.

From the high ground at Rossal, one can see the red roof and white walls of Patrick Sellar's two-storey house at Syre. Not far from it are the small kirk of Syre, with its red corrugated-iron roof, the war memorial and the junction of the B871 that runs east across the moors to Kinbrace.

The population of Farr decreased by four hundred between 1790 and 1831. Apart from six hundred acres on the coast, where the resettled evictees had their small fields, and eight hundred or so acres of woods, the whole parish was turned over to sheep. In 1831 there were 418 families and 22,000 sheep, and only 24 families lived inland.

In 1884, at the height of the agitation over crofters' rights and the excitement surrounding the new Franchise Bill, the descendants of the evicted tenants staged a triumphant march up the strath. Organized by the Strathnaver Crofters' Association, whose chairman was the Free Church minister Donald Mackenzie, the marchers numbered almost two thousand and came from all over the north coast. The day of the march, Tuesday 14 October, dawned under a leaden sky and threatened rain but, as the procession entered the strath, the sun broke through the cloud like an omen of a bright future. Flags flew from every house; bagpipes were pressed into exultant service. A student called Angus Mackay rode from Bettyhill east to meet marchers coming from Strathy and Armadale, carrying a fiery cross. The men's hats were decorated with banners in Gaelic and English with legends such as 'Crofts on Strathnaver' and 'Land reform'. Larger banners read 'Farr demands the Highlands for Highlanders, and a vote for all householders' and

'Who would be free, must himself strike the first blow.' Some carried spades or drove carts with ploughs and harrows as symbols of their protest. The river was in spate, and it took some time for the mass of people to cross it by the chain-boat (the bridge was yet to be built at Invernaver). Some men plunged in and swam their horses over. One of the marchers was an eighty-six-year-old woman, Grizel Macdonald, who had been evicted from Langdale as a young girl; she took with her a sieve with a rim made from Strathnaver wood and was described as walking proudly. The procession went up the strath as far as a flat meadow opposite Skelpick, where speeches were made from a wagonette loaned for the occasion by the owner of the Bettyhill Hotel. A letter from the Marquis of Stafford, the son of the Duke of Sutherland and at the time a supporter of land reform, was read out: the Marquis regretted his absence but wished the gathering 'every success'.

It was the last time Strathnaver saw such a number of folk. They won the right to vote in Parliamentary elections, and eventually the Crofter Acts gave them security of tenure on their crofts, but Strathnaver remains to this day largely free of people.

At the head of the strath, in an area with many standing stones, hut circles and cairns, the river and the road bend westward. Loch Naver is a long and beautiful body of water, and at its western end the B873 joins the A836 to bring the traveller to the village of Altnaharra.

An attractive place, Altnaharra sits on a broad shelf of land between the Rivers Mudale and Vagastie which feed Loch Naver from the west. This is a meeting of the ways and a stopping place. The A836 from Tongue to Lairg crosses the road from Strathnaver to Strathmore, and it is also the halfway point between Lairg and the north coast. The Altnaharra Hotel, more or less in the centre of the scattered village, began life in about 1820 as a coaching inn but it was not long before the potential of the area for game fishing was realized. The hotel's angling records go back to 1886, and the bar has many interesting relics of the sport. In the 1930s up to thirty gillies and farm workers owed their livelihood to the hotel. Then guests had to bring their own fresh vegetables with them; now the freezer has relieved them of this responsibility, leaving them to think only of the trout and salmon in the lochs and burns.

The ruins of Ardvreck Castle beside Loch Assynt.

The pier at Lochinver.

Decorating pots at Highland Stoneware, Lochinver.

The caves near Inchnadamph, where this journey ends.

The A836 runs south from Altnaharra through Strath Vagastie and past the Crask, where there is another inn, to Lairg. The eastern side of the Strath is dominated by the massive ridge of Ben Klibreck, rising to over 3,150 feet in the peak of Meall nan Con. The moors to the west of the strath are lower but are riven by burns and bogland; the craggy Ben Hee, the highest mountain in this region, reaches almost to 2,900 feet above the small Loch a'Ghorm-choire, but most of the country is considerably lower. Patches of forest break the skyline and add splashes of green to the browns and blues.

Going west from Bettyhill on the main coast road, one comes on the River Borgie. There are extensive stands of coniferous trees in the valley here. Borgie Forest, now part of the larger Naver Forest, dates from 1920, the first Forestry Commission plantation in the Highlands, on land gifted to the Crown by the Duke of Sutherland. The road north along the west bank of the Borgie leads the traveller to the crofting townships of Skerray and the beach at the west end of Torrisdale Bay. Skerray is the site of an active community co-operative, where the crofters have worked to drain and reclaim bogland for productive agriculture. The tenants of the area also operate a collective animal feed scheme and have even collaborated on a video film of their way of life.

From the harbour at Skerray one can see the bare, rocky islet of Eilean Neave, whose name indicates that, despite its inhospitable appearance, it was once home for some monks or a hermit. A plaque on the harbour wall at Skerray commemorates two men, Hector Mackay and John Anderson, who were lost at sea in March 1973, when their boat was destroyed in a storm while they were fishing for lobsters; only the vessel's petrol tank was found, washed up on South Ronaldsay in Orkney, it is said.

Eilean nan Ron's story is similar to that of Stroma. Until a few decades ago, the three-square-mile island supported several crofting families. Although winter storms could interrupt boat crossings to Skerray for as much as two weeks, life on the island is remembered by those who once lived there as pleasant and happy. In 1937 the people moved to the mainland. Sheep are still grazed on the island.

At Coldbackie we get our first view of the Kyle of Tongue. The road curves around the flank of the steep heathery hill called Cnoc an Fhreiceadain (the name again refers to it as a watchtower) and suddenly allows the traveller to see the broad mouth of the Kyle, at low tide a tapestry of golden sand and blue-green water, with the cluster of rocky islets called the Rabbit Islands athwart its jaws. The A838 sweeps across the Kyle just to the north of Tongue on a causeway opened in 1971. Before that the main road followed the shore up to Kinloch and then down the west side before turning up over the moors of the Moine.

Tongue itself is a large village, spread, in two lines mainly, along the braeside on the east shore of the Kyle. The church here was built in 1724, on the site of two former churches, and in its vaults lie buried several members of the Mackay family. The chiefs of Clan Mackay had their home here, and the family loft was removed from the church to the National Museum of Antiquities in Edinburgh only in 1960.

Opposite the village, on a knoll thrusting seaward, stand the remains of Castle Bharraich. A path from the village leads up to it, or it can be reached from the bridge across the Rhian Burn; either route through the birchwoods and the tall bracken can in summer be a clammy experience. The castle is a simple, four-square ruin, standing maybe twenty feet high; a natural rock wall cuts across the peninsula behind it on the landward side, and there are indentations in the ground on the seaward side that could mark where a ditch was cut. From the castle you can see out through the mouth of the Kyle. The history of the place is obscure. Its building is sometimes attributed to the Norsemen, but others consider the fifteenth century a likelier birthdate.

Down close to the causeway but hidden by woods and walls is Tongue House, the home of the Countess of Sutherland. It was built in 1678 and was described by a traveller in the 1790s as a 'beautiful spot, laid out with gardens, surrounded with beautiful trees'. Not far from it and hard by the main road is a youth hostel. Tongue House was built on the ashes of its predecessor, which was burned in 1654, most probably by Cromwell's army while in pursuit of Lord Reay, the Chief of Mackay, who had risen in arms in support of Charles II, though Ian Grimble in his book *Chief of Mackay* suggests that Reay may have torched his home himself to deny it to the enemy.

This Lord Reay was the second to hold the title. His father had been granted it earlier in the century; before that the leaders of the

Mackays had been simply and grandly chiefs. The first Lord Reay died in 1649. A few months later, at the end of January 1649, Charles I went to the block in Whitehall. The execution of their king horrified the people of Scotland. Reay and the Mackenzies raised some seven hundred men in the royalist cause and occupied Inverness twice, first in February 1650, when they stayed for only a short time, and again in May with a larger force and a more determined plan: a local minister recorded the event, '... the Lord Ray and the Mackenzies mustered and made a body of 1500; and coming over, some at Cessock, some at Beauly, crossed the bridge at Ness uppon the Lord's day in time of Divine service and alarmed the people of Inverness, impeding God's worship in that town....' The wild Highlandmen, for so they would have been seen by the douce burghers, forced their hosts to lay out food for them and, when the meat proved tough, are said to have charged their providers with compensation for the wear and tear on their teeth.

The army marched east as far as Balveny Castle, where the village of Dufftown is now, to join forces with the royalist commander-in-chief, Middleton, but they were attacked by Parliamentary cavalry who had made a surprise night march over the moors. In the battle, four hundred royalists were killed and Lord Reay himself was captured. He was imprisoned in Edinburgh Castle and, under threat of execution, was forced to sign blank bonds as compensation for the damage done to the property of the Grays of Sutherland. The Estates, as the Scottish Parliament was called, commanded that his incarceration continue until all his debts were paid.

The Earl of Sutherland, long an enemy of the house of Mackay, did not miss this opportunity. In February 1649 he had petitioned the Estates for assistance in dealing with the raiding of the Mackays: he claimed that four hundred men were needed to guard his land against the incursions of his northern neighbours and that Lord Reay, before the death of his father, had withheld rents due to the Earl from Strathnaver. The Estates granted the Earl authority to garrison a fort in Strathnaver to keep the Mackays in order: it was built in June 1649, a horseshoe-shaped rampart close to the Burn of Langdale. Now, in August 1650, with Lord Reay safely behind bars, the Earl put in a claim for compensation of £20,935.6s.8d.

Two months before, Charles II had landed at the mouth of the Spey, officially King of Scots. In September, however, Cromwell's army defeated the royalists at Dunbar and advanced on Edinburgh, and at this point Lord Reay effected a remarkable escape from his prison, aided by his wife – 'the mirror of our north bred ladyes, the prettiest, wittiest woman that I ever knew here', in the words of one contemporary. During the escape, a giant, hook-nosed Mackay called John Abrach laid out his master's guards and delayed pursuit, only to be captured: Cromwell, impressed by the clansman's display of selfless courage, took one look at John Abrach's craggy face and pardoned him.

At the end of 1650 Charles and the Estates met at Perth and planned a new campaign against the Lord Protector. Hew Mackay was dispatched to raise forces in Strathnaver, and the Earl of Sutherland's fort in Strathnaver was taken off the public purse. In April 1651 the Mackays marched south again in the royal cause, to Stirling and then into England – only to be defeated at Worcester in September. Charles II fled the country, and the Parliamentary Army occupied all Scotland to quench once and for all the flames of rebellion.

Success did not come quickly, however, for in 1654 Middleton occupied Dornoch, and Lord Reay brought two hundred men to join him there, in the episode already described in Chapter 3. Retreating from Dornoch, Middleton's army passed by Wick and Girnigoe Castle, where the Earl of Caithness had taken up a strong defensive position. In July 1654 Middleton was finally defeated in a battle at Dalnaspidal near Drumochter, but Reay, who had left his army when it had passed through Strathnaver, kept the field until May 1656, when a settlement negotiated with Cromwell was finally put into effect and the clan chief was pardoned for his long royalist campaign.

(It is remarkable that, between October 1653 and September 1656, John Neilson Abrach of Strathnaver, disdaining to take part in national wars, raided the west of Caithness at least seven times in a freebooting campaign of his own.)

Later in the seventeenth century, Lord Lovat paid a visit to the Chief of Mackay at Durness, and the account of the celebrations gives a vivid picture of this last outpost of the Gaelic society that had once flourished throughout the chiefdoms of the

Highlands and islands. 'The Lord Reay contrived all maner of sport and recreation to divert his dear Lovat ... sometimes out at sea in berges afishing, sometimes haukeing and hunting, sometimes arching at buts and bowmarks, jumping, wrestling, dancing.... All the gentlemen conveened, and so to the deer hunting, for my Lord Reay hath the finest and richest forest in the kingdom for deer and reas [roes], their number and nimbleness.' Lovat stayed for over a month in this sporting paradise and returned with many gifts, including a horse, 'several excellent firelocks, bowes and a sword', two deerhounds, a silk plaid woven by Lady Reay herself, and an escort of twenty men as far as the bounds of Sutherland. It is also recorded that Reay kept a piper, a harper and a fool, and a tutor for his family. It is obvious that the depredations of the wars had not depleted the family standard of living too much, and it is ironic that they managed to come through the turbulence of the seventeenth century to meet a quieter, but more devastating, demise later.

In 1679–81 a court action annulled the effects of the blank bonds signed in 1650. The legal brain behind this move was Sir George Munro of Culrain, who was the commander of all government forces in 'North Britain' and, incidentally, the Master of Reay's father-in-law. At the same time the Master rebuilt Tongue House: a plaque in the wall bears his initials 'DR' and the crest and motto of the Mackays – 'Manu forti', 'With a strong hand'.

In July 1745 George, the third Lord Reay, and William, Earl of Sutherland, signed a bond of friendship that put a formal end to the centuries of feuding that had riven the fabric of life in Sutherland: '... from henceforth we shall bury in everlasting oblivion all differences and misunderstandings that may have unhapplie taken place between us.'

The demise of the Mackay family came early in the nineteenth century and, in keeping with the way life had changed, not by the sword but through the bank balance. Eric, the seventh Lord Reay, gradually fell deeper and deeper into debt and, in 1829, sold his entire estate to the Countess of Sutherland for £300,000. 'Thus what the Mackays held through sunshine and through storm for about twenty generations was at last miserably frittered away ... by a degenerate son,' wrote Angus Mackay in his history *The Book of Mackay*. The Countess had already, in

1813, acquired the Strathy estate, and in 1830 the Mackays of Bighouse sold Strath Halladale to her. The Mackay chief owned no land at all in his home country.

At Tongue the A836 bends south and runs through the hills to Altnaharra. For miles the route is dominated by Ben Loyal, whose highest peak is 2,504 feet. The name is better spelt 'Laoghal' and is derived from the Gaelic for calf, perhaps a reference to the old practice of pasturing cattle on the hills in summer. In 1841 the Reverend Hugh Mackenzie wrote of it as 'this noble hill, the queen of Scottish mountains'. 'On a summer morning,' he went on, 'or after a sweet summer shower, when the transparent mist is reposing on its bosom, or coiling among its peaks, the appearance ... is very beautiful and often singularly fantastic.' Most pictures of the mountain are taken from Kinloch, at the head of the Kyle, whence the elegant ridge is viewed to advantage. I first climbed it from the east side, from the road by Loch Loyal. It is not a difficult ascent, and the traverse of the ridge affords superb views across the entire north.

At the south end of Loch Loyal the road bends like an elbow around the lonely, now uninhabited house of Inchkinloch before climbing up towards Altnaharra and the head of Strathnaver. A road sign at Inchkinloch tells us: 'Lambs have no road sense.' The motorist will probably already have discovered that sheep can be a traffic hazard. The old ewes have little fear of cars but the season's lambs are unaccustomed to the noise and are very skittish.

The country around Tongue and the head of the Kyle is a fascinating mixture of woodland and moor, too easily missed by those who drive west across the causeway. A short distance beyond where the old road dips across the Rhian Burn there is a monument, a short granite pillar in memory of Ewen Robertson, a local poet and politician who was overcome on this spot in a blizzard in 1895. Robertson was a witness at the inquiry of the Napier Commission in 1884, and in his verses he spoke against the landlordism that had cleared the land of its people. The stone bears two of his lines with an English translation:

> 'N ait nan caorach bithidh tuath
> Crodh-laoigh air airgh 'n ait damh ruadh;

In place of the sheep there will be people,
Cattle at the shielings in place of stags.

Close by, near the farm of Ribigill, one can see the foundations
and the little parks of Scrabster, a deserted village.

Two miles further south, between the road and Ben Loyal, lies
a glimmering bowl of water – Lochan Hakel. At the south-east
corner of the lochan there is an intriguing survival of some
mysterious neolithic sculpture: on the top of a large boulder on
the shore are cup and ring markings. The rings, ground in the
stone, are about four inches across, and the entire surface
resembles a mini-lunar landscape with craters. The purpose of
these marks, which are found elsewhere in Scotland, is unknown.
Opposite the boulder, on a little islet, is a small drystone
building. Called Grianan, not much is known about this place
but Kevin O'Reilly, in a brochure on local antiquities, suggests it
is a Celtic fort dating from around the time of Christ.

To the east of Lochan Hakel a long ridge of heather stretches
towards Ben Loyal. It was here, in 1433, that a fierce battle
between the Mackays and the forces of the Earl of Sutherland
was fought; the conflict takes its name from the ridge, 'the ridge
of the cup', Druim na Cupa in Gaelic.

The Chief of the Mackays at the time was called Angus Dubh.
He probably became chief in 1406 after the battle of Tuiteam
Tarbhach and the death of his uncle Hugh. According to Robert
Mackay's history of the clan, published in 1829, Angus had four
thousand men at his command – a force to be reckoned with in
the interclan feuding of the Middle Ages – and it was not long
before he was in action against Donald, Lord of the Isles. The
latter claimed the earldom of Ross (his wife was a sister of the
late Earl of Ross, whose only child had become a nun) and to
advance his prospects he laid waste a swathe of countryside
along the Ross-Sutherland border. In the course of this campaign
Donald probably destroyed Mackay property. Angus's forces met
the invader in battle, perhaps at Dingwall, but were defeated;
Angus Dubh himself was taken prisoner. He was later forced into
a marriage with Elizabeth, Donald's sister, perhaps as part of a
peace treaty between the clans, before he returned to his own
country in Strathnaver.

In 1420 James I summoned the Highland chiefs to meet him at

Inverness in an attempt to end the guerrilla wars raging in the north. Two chiefs were tried and summarily beheaded, and others were taken hostage as guarantees of good behaviour from their relatives. Among the latter was Angus's son, Neil, who spent a period on the Bass Rock in the Firth of Forth, thereby gaining the nickname that he would carry for the rest of his life – Neil Bhass. With his son incarcerated, Angus, now an old man, feared he would die without an heir, and he favoured one of his illegitimate offspring, Ian Abrach, to succeed him. His decision was opposed by other Mackays who felt themselves to have a prior claim to the chieftainship. The Earl of Sutherland lent his support to the rival claimants, and an army marched north towards Tongue to depose Angus.

The loyal Mackays chose to meet the invaders at Druim na Cupa. Ian Abrach positioned his men on the slopes and in a wood, and insisted that his elderly father watch the battle from the safety of Ben Loyal. The conflict was fierce and without quarter, but when a Mackay detachment assaulted the invaders from the rear, they faltered, their leaders fell and those who could began to flee. The Mackays pursued them, cutting them down in the heather. But it was not a total victory: Angus Dubh came down from his watching place to see the battlefield, and a Sutherland, lying hidden, shot him with an arrow. The wound was mortal.

On the death of his father, Ian Abrach took over the mantle of chief. For a while, it is said, he lived in a cave near Castle Bharraich to escape the assassins of the Earl of Sutherland. In 1437 Neil Bhass escaped from his prison and came north to claim his rightful title. Ian Abrach 'resigned' the chieftainship and went to live at Achness in Strathnaver, where he fathered a string of descendants who kept the practices of plunder and raid alive for several generations.

The western side of the Kyle of Tongue is largely bare moorland. Only at the seaward tip are there many houses, comprising the crofting townships of Midtown, Skinnet, Talmine, Achnahuaigh and Strathen, past Melness House. Strathen has a fine beach, and the rocky creek of Portvasgo is a salmon-fishing station. The Rabbit Islands lie just offshore here; at low tide a spit of sand connects them to the headland of Ard Skinid, and it was here that a remarkable incident in the '45

Rebellion was played out.

In January 1746 the Jacobites had captured at Montrose a government sloop called *Hazard* and had renamed her *Prince Charles*. In March the *Prince Charles* sailed from France with money and stores for the rebel army, by this time falling back on Inverness. Off Troup Head she was spotted by the frigate HMS *Sheerness*, which pursued her through the Pentland Firth and finally caught up with her off the Kyle on 29 March. Her captain knew that the sandbanks across the Kyle would prevent the larger frigate from following them into the sheltered water, but he made an error of judgement himself, and the *Prince Charles* drove aground at Ard Skinid. Stuck fast on an ebbing tide, the sloop was pounded by the *Sheerness*'s broadsides until the frigate retired to deeper water. The *Prince Charles* was now a wreck, almost awash, many of her crew dead or wounded, and the captain decided to abandon her, intending to carry the Jacobite supplies overland. Under the safety of night, laden with gear, the men set off along the shore of the Kyle and came to Melness House, then occupied by a Mackay who fortunately for them was the only Jacobite sympathizer in the area. On the following day the fugitives moved further south to Kinloch and round to Lochan Hakel.

They walked into an ambush. What they had not known was that some eighty men of Lord Loudon's regiment were at that time at Tongue House, whither they had retreated from Dornoch some days before. Lord Reay, his son and some other guests led Loudon's soldiers to the attack, cheered by this chance for some action. After a short fight, near Druim na Cupa as it happened, in which three or four rebels were killed and only one man wounded on the other side, the rebels were overwhelmed. Arms and chests of bullion destined for Prince Charles were captured: although one chest disappeared and another was broken into, the sum taken was reckoned at 12,500 guineas. There are many stories, however, of *louis d'or* finding local currency, and according to some sources the sum landed at Ard Skinid had been closer to £27,000.

Between the Kyle of Tongue and Loch Eriboll, the A838 crosses the Moine, a high, rough, empty stretch of country to which, James Hall thought in 1807, criminals could be transported instead of to Botany Bay. The road across the moors was not laid until 1830; the foundations were floated on bundles of heather sunk in the morass, and a house of refuge was built midway to provide shelter for travellers caught in bad weather. Moine House still has a plaque on its wall to commemorate the efforts of the road-builders. The moors extend right to the coast between Strathen and Hope and break suddenly in a cliff wall in places almost nine hundred feet high. The rocks are greyish in colour, giving the name of Whiten Head, or An Ceann Geal in Gaelic, to the promontory bounding the eastern entrance to Loch Eriboll.

From the little hamlet of Hope (the name is from a Gaelic word for bay), nestling in a narrow, wooded valley, a road runs inland along Loch Hope. Single-tracked, with grass growing through the tarmac in places, the road skirts the brooding, often mist-shrouded mass of Ben Hope, the most northerly Munro in Scotland at 3,040 feet, and runs up through Strath More to emerge onto a broad, grassy plateau before descending to Altnaharra.

The upper part of Strathmore is secluded, its flat floor curtained by hills on both sides. In the centre of the strath is the shell of the best-preserved broch in the county – Dun Dornaigill. The drystone wall of the broch varies in height from about six feet to over twenty and forms a ring, close to the road on a brae above the meandering river. The entrance through the ring is blocked but the massive triangular lintel above the door is a memorable tribute to the mason's skill. Towards the end of the eighteenth century the skeletons of two men, one over seven feet tall, are reported to have been dug up here; unfortunately the bones on being exposed to the air 'mouldered into dust'. The broch commands the entrance to the narrowest part of the strath and is close to the confluence of several routes to the south. The farm of Altnacaillich is just to the north; the strath was once much more heavily peopled.

The A838 winds along the eastern shore of Loch Eriboll, dipping past the wooded, green vales of the farms of Kempie and Eriboll, descending slowly to the flat pastures of Strath Beg at the head of the loch. The great crags of Creag na Faoilinn and Creag Shomlairle rear up above the little strath in an impressive escarpment, in contrast to the steady, gentle slopes on the western side of Loch Eriboll that culminate in the long ridge of

Beinn Spionnaidh. Eilean Choraidh lies in the middle of the loch like a long, green seal. There are some ruins on it, perhaps associated with the limekilns said to have been established here by Lord Reay in the late eighteenth century.

The long line of crofts on the west side of the loch makes up the district of Laid. Near the mouth of the loch is the little harbour of Rispond. Now privately owned, it still has the buildings (complete with outside staircase, crow-stepped gables and fish weathervane) erected when a herring and salmon fishery was developed here in the nineteenth century. From the heights along this stretch of the coast, there is a fine view of the scarred, truncated bulk of Whiten Head.

Cliffs, stacks and sandy beaches alternate and mingle along the shoreline west of Rispond. The road passes through Sangobeg and Leirinmore before cresting a brae to descend to Smoo.

The great cave at Smoo is one of the most awesome natural features on the northern coast. It is easily reached. In fact, the A838 crosses its roof, and a good path leads down to the floor of the Geodha Smoo, the long geo that connects the cavern to the sea. On the east face of the geo, sheep tracks criss-cross the braeside like the stitches in a guernsey, and on the grass visitors have laid out stones to make a kind of grafitti – initials, a heart etc. The outer chamber of the cave has a huge, vaulted roof, like a cathedral, with a hole open to the sky, and echoes to the cackling of fulmars and the thundering of the burn, Allt Smoo, plummeting through a sinkhole into an inner chamber. To see the Allt Smoo, from above as it were, it is necessary to cross the main road; the water froths and roars, when the burn is in spate, as it flashes under a natural arch at one side of the sinkhole.

The cave has drawn the attention of travellers for centuries and may have been used as a permanent place of habitation in prehistoric times. Worked stone and bones have been exposed here by erosion. The honour of the first exploration of its inner recesses was claimed by Lord Reay in the seventeenth century. Reay took six attendants and a piper with him but, goes the story, only he and the piper reappeared; neither would tell what had happened, and neither was ever again seen to smile. A dog that accompanied them later turned up in a small cave two miles inland, its hair scraped from its body in its struggle to get out.

Sir Walter Scott and a party took a boat into the cave in 1814;

Scott's impressions are recorded in his book *Northern Lights*. Jim Johnston of Bettyhill and two companions took a rubber dinghy inside in 1980 and described the experience in the *John O'Groat Journal*: 'A moment's paddling took us to the centre of the flooded chamber.... Through a hole in the roof, into the semi-darkness below, poured the Allt Smoo, the roar of its fall ruling our speech.' Less adventurous visitors can glimpse the shimmering fall of the burn through the cleft that links the outer and inner chambers. Beyond the fall and its pool, there is a third chamber. Here, Jim Johnston found that the light and the sound of the fall dwindled into nothing, and he and his friends had to proceed very carefully along the tube-like, thirty-yard tunnel to the 'well' at the far end. They found floating in the pool a Coke bottle, and an eel swimming casually around.

The word Smoo may be derived from the Norse *smuga*, a hole, but this cave is a deal more than such a description would imply. Visitors should not be tempted to penetrate too far into its gloom without advice. Jim Johnston found that the water-level in the chambers could rise rapidly and dramatically with heavy rain in the outside world.

The large village of Durness spreads itself across high ground around Sango Bay. A long loop of the A838 encompasses the valley of the burn draining Loch Caladil, with the church at its apex; a minor road, with a vicious gradient at the east end, cuts across the burn valley and offers a shortcut. In the centre of Durness, the main road bends southward and runs down to the Kyle and Keoldale.

The peninsula of Faraid Head juts northward from Durness. On the western side there are long acres of dunes fringing a fine beach, open to the sea and the cliffs of the Parph and a great place from which to watch the sun set on a summer night. Perhaps it was the physical attractions of the sea and the clear, glancing light that led St Maolrubha to choose this spot for the founding of the second Christian church in Sutherland early in the eighth century. Balnakeil kirk, now a ruin, stands on the same site, surrounded by its cemetery, at the root of the peninsula. Balnakeil House, built as a residence of the Mackay chiefs in the mid-eighteenth century, is close by, but the church predates it by a couple of generations. There is a tradition that Bishop Gilbert de Moravia opened a gold mine here in the thirteenth century. There is no firm evidence to back up this claim, but the kirk at Balnakeil was supplying oil and incense to Dornoch at that time. The present ruin is what remains of the last church built by Lord Reay in 1619. The date is visible above the unusual tomb in the south wall. It contains the dust of a notorious highwayman, and the inscription on the slab gives his name and a summary of his character:

> Donald MakMurchou hier lyis lo
> vas il to his freind, var to his fo
> true to his maister in veird and vo.*

The story goes that Donald offered £1,000 to Lord Reay to help finance the rebuilding of the kirk, on the condition that this vault be provided for him so that his enemies could not desecrate his remains. The walls of the kirk make an L-shape, not large but well proportioned and pleasing. The entrance has a bell niche above it, with a sundial to let the ringer know the time, and ivy grows thickly on the south side.

The churchyard contains a monument, erected in 1827, to Rob Donn Mackay. This great Gaelic poet was born in the now-gone village of Muisel near Altnacaillich in Strathmore in 1714. According to the Reverend Donald Sage, Mackay 'looked into the face of nature, with a poet's eye'. 'When he composed a song he no sooner sang it than, with all the speed of the press, it circulated throughout the country.' An edition of his work was published in 1829, but the editor, trying to improve the poet's dialect, 'strangled his poetry' in Sage's opinion. Another writer, Donald Mackay, thought that it was impossible to translate his songs 'with a tolerable degree of taste'. Alas, there is no up-to-date edition of Rob Donn's poetry, either in Gaelic or in translation, but excerpts can be found, such as this one in Derick Thomson's *An Introduction to Gaelic Poetry*. The verse is from a poem called '*Na Casagan Dubha*', 'The Black Cassocks', attacking the proscription of Highland dress by Act of Parliament in 1747, but its words have a modern ring to them:

> I am saddened by Scotland!
> You've shown clearly your motives;

* var = worse, veird = word, vo = deed.

your mind is divided,
which has spoilt any venture.
The Government read
greed in those who had turned to them,
and gave avarice bait
till you tore at each other.

Donn composed love songs, religious poetry, barbed satire – the whole gamut of the art – and he remained illiterate all his life, dying in 1777 at the age of sixty-four. His gravestone, not far from his monument and close to the kirk door, is a simple, pale grey slab bearing just his name – ROBERT DONN – and the year.

There are many interesting tombstones in Balnakeil kirkyard. From one we discover that James Anderson of Keoldale married twice, outliving both wives but writing poignant epitaphs to record his loss. Ann, his first wife, died in 1783; she was only thirty-two but she was 'Ten years the genuine copy/ of a virtuous wife/ Clear was the prospid of her landing safely/ from the storms of life.' His second wife, Fairly, died seven years later at the even young age of twenty-seven: 'Though mother and stepmother/ when but scarce nineteen/ in both relations she/ did eminently shine/ Esteemed of every rank/ while Maid or Wife/ Now Angel Bright/ She quaffs immortal life.'

Not far from Balnakeil kirk, between it and Durness proper, is the Balnakeil Craft Village. A bright, cheerful place, it is the only craft village in Britain to be owned by its occupants; pets and children play in the grassy spaces between the buildings. As well as pursuing their individual arts and crafts, the residents formed a community co-operative in 1983 and now operate a bus service to Ullapool and Tongue, a visitors' centre and community programmes in association with the Manpower Services Commission. The minibus service to Cape Wrath was a brainwave of a founding resident at Balnakeil. The village was set up by the Sutherland County Council in the early 1960s when they bought derelict Air Ministry buildings for £3,000 and offered them to craftspeople. It was a bold, imaginative scheme but not without its detractors; some of the staider residents of the county grumbled and looked askance at what they anticipated would be an influx of drop-outs and ne'er-do-wells.

Their forebodings were not realized, and now the village is an established part of local life. The craftspeople, numbering approximately twenty, and their families play active roles in the community.

Craftspeople are often regarded with suspicion in the north, feelings not always unjustified, for some have come without much idea of what is required of them and have not lasted long. However, the crafts industries are important in the Highland economy: in 1980 a survey revealed that they were employing some seven thousand people in Highland areas, earning for the Region over £20 million. The statistics do not bring out another point – perhaps more important in the long run: that the incomers are usually young people determined to make a go of something in areas bled by depopulation for many decades.

The Kyle of Durness forms a winding, shallow arm of the sea between Durness and Cape Wrath. From Keoldale, a little ferry crosses the water. Low tide leaves bare great expanses of sand, through which the rivers from the moors twist, claret-coloured, seaward. Seals haul themselves out to bask on the beaches. From the pier on the west side of the Kyle, a narrow road runs high above the shore before turning west at Achiemore to cross a rolling moor of grass and peathags to the Cape. The district is called the Parph, and it comprises about eighty square miles of empty country. No one lives here now, but the last crofting family left only about sixteen years ago. There was once a school at Achiemore. No private vehicles are allowed on the Cape Wrath road, though one can take a bicycle across on the ferry. The minibuses that take the tourists up to the lighthouse are floated across by their operators on special rafts.

Just to the east of Cape Wrath, divided from it by the secluded cove of Kearvaig, is Clo Mor: reaching close to nine hundred feet, it is the highest cliff on the British mainland. The Cape itself is dramatic and cliff-bound. Off the point, a black, foam-lashed rock called Duslic sticks up like a kist in the sea, the last piece of permanently exposed land. No name would seem more appropriate for this windy corner than the English word 'wrath', but in fact the name is derived from the Norse *hvarf*, meaning a turning point – for a mariner, a very apposite name. The word 'Parph' comes from the same source.

'On this dread Cape, so fatal to mariners, it is proposed to build a lighthouse and Mr Stevenson has fixed on an advantageous situation,' wrote Sir Walter Scott during his visit in 1814. 'It is a high promontory, with steep sides that go sheer down to the breakers, which lash its feet. There is no landing except in a small creek about a mile and a half to the eastward. There the foam of the sea plays at long bowls with a huge collection of large stones, some of them a ton in weight, but which these fearful billows chuck up and down as a child tosses a ball.' The lighthouse was eventually built in 1827.

Access to the Cape Wrath peninsula by road is not without hazard. Over eight thousand acres are used by the Royal Navy and the RAF as a weapons-testing area. Malcolm Spaven in his book *Fortress Scotland* refers to the Cape as the only ship-to-shore bombardment range in Europe, and says that NATO and non-NATO navies practise shelling targets up to two miles inland. Sheep are sometimes victims, and local people have been wounded on occasion. The RAF practise live bombing on the islet of An Garbh-eilean. The Ordnance Survey map has 'DANGER AREA' in red letters printed across the Cape Wrath road. Visitors should take careful note. Seven or eight times a year, military exercises interrupt the bus service to the Cape – needless to add, causing some annoyance to local people.

9

The West Coast

The cliffs and geos for several miles south of Cape Wrath are accessible only on foot. To see the little bay of Keisgaig, the loch behind the sand dunes at Sandwood Bay and the valley, Strath Shinary, that runs down to it, one has to take one of the two paths that lead north from the crofting districts near Kinlochbervie. This wilderness of moorland rises to its greatest heights in a number of peaks such as Creag Riabhach and Fashven.

The A838, running straight south-westward from Durness, skirts the area on its way to Rhiconich. This road reaches no great height. Near where the hill of Farrmheall rises like a dark sentinel, there is a well. It consists of an iron trough set in stone, the metal painted yellow, and above it a plaque that reads '1833. As a mark of gratitude and respect to the inhabitants of Durness and Eddrachillis for their hospitality while projecting this road this inscription is placed over this well by their humble servant Peter Lawson surveyor.' The view from the well takes in the broad slash of Strath Dionard running into the hills between Beinn Spionnaidh and Foinaven.

The view northward looks down the valley of the Dionard towards the Kyle of Durness. The river meanders through its broad, green plain. In contrast to the hills around it, the valley appears lush, especially in sunshine. Once, however, on a June day, I had to shelter from a hailstorm at Gualin House, two miles south of Lawson's well. Built early in the 1880s, Gualin House is the only dwelling on this long stretch of road. The name means 'shoulder' in Gaelic, and it has also been adopted for a Nature Conservancy Council reserve, running to over six thousand acres, that encompasses the ridges of Foinaven and part of Strath Dionard.

Foinaven and its neighbouring peaks, Arkle and Ben Stack, are rugged, broken masses of rock, hills for the experienced climber or walker: they dominate the country at the head of Loch Inchard. At Rhiconich there is a mountain rescue post.

Parts of the B801 from Rhiconich to Kinlochbervie are good, two-lane highway, in contrast to many of the single-track A roads in the north-west. The reason is fish. Lorries rumble continuously to and from Kinlochbervie to transport the catches landed there to distant markets.

The small town is scattered about on a hilly peninsula called Cnoc na h-Eannaichie on the north side of Loch Inchard. Dating from 1886, the old pier, wooden and decaying gently, is at the head of Loch Clash on the Atlantic side of the Cnoc, but the new harbour is tucked into the sheltered east end. The modern development of Kinlochbervie began in about 1970, and now it is a very busy place. Although there are only three locally owned boats, some fifty vessels crowd into the anchorage, tied up one to the other along the concrete quays. They are nearly all east-coast boats, registered, for example, in Banff or Fraserburgh and having names like *Achilles, Apollo, Bon Ami, Olive Leaf, Crystal Tide* and *Bountiful*. On several occasions, four thousand boxes of fish have been landed here in one night: four years ago, one thousand boxes was cause for comment. The east-coast men come in from the sea on Thursday and drive home for the weekend, right across Scotland to their home ports in Buchan, returning on Sunday to fish the western seas again. The Minch and waters around and to the west of the Hebrides are now Scotland's most important fishing ground. Foreign boats come here too, and the conservation of stocks, particularly in the face of EEC regulations on quotas, is a pressing problem. Harbour improvements are still planned at Kinlochbervie: there is not enough room for all the boats who wish to use it, and the place has a frontier air where the earth-moving machines are crunching up the reddish rocks to make way for new quays and buildings.

At the head of the bay, not far from the bustle of the harbour, stands the Free Presbyterian kirk, another of Telford's buildings.

In its yard a tomb of red boulders marks the last resting place of Robert Stronach, an honorary Brigadier General and the proprietor of the Kinlochbervie estate in the 1920s. At the eastern end of the town, close to Loch Innis na Ba'Buidhe, one can see a house with a remarkable, futuristic-looking mural on its two-storey gable. This is the Free Presbyterian manse, and the artist is the minister, a fact that may surprise those with preconceived notions of this denomination's austere Calvinism. Brilliant colours, abstract motifs and symbols such as Noah's rainbow and the Tree of Life make up the striking composition.

Beyond Kinlochbervie, the crofting districts of Oldshoremore, Oldshorebeg, Droman, Blairmore, Balchrick and Sheigra succeed each other along the road until one is facing the open Atlantic. The coast is rocky and desolate but cups within its surf-gnawed fingers crescents of clean sand that sparkle beside the green sea. Off the coast, rocks and islets stick up like crumbs around the edge of a plate.

The whole of the north-west corner of Sutherland used to comprise the parish of Durness, but in 1724 the General Assembly of the Church of Scotland divided the area into three parishes. The boundaries of the new parish of Eddrachilis (the name is Gaelic for 'between two kyles') were fixed almost at Cape Wrath in the north and at Klyesku in the south. It has always been a sparsely populated area – a look at the landscape shows clearly the reason for this. Dr Webster's census in 1755 numbered '869 souls'. The number rose to well over a thousand by 1790 but decreased again after evictions and dearth drove people to emigrate. The minister noted in the 1790s that there were 'no less than 8 different burying grounds' because of the rough roads and the distances coffins had to be carried. Life was very hard then, but the minister found his parishioners to be excellent boatmen '... and ready to learn any mechanical business; so that scarcely any artificers in the parish are but self-taught'. Black cattle and the speckled Galloway sheep were kept; goats and horses were reared. 'There have been of late years,' wrote the minister, 'several poets in this parish, whose compositions, mostly of the lyric kind, have been admired by good judges, and have shown them to be possessed of uncommon parts and genius.'

Twenty years before, the naturalist Thomas Pennant wrote very strongly of what he found in Assynt, just to the south:

'... the people [are] almost torpid with idleness, and most wretched: their hovels most miserable, made of poles wattled and covered with thin sods.' Although he recognized the drawbacks of the climate, he harshly judged the people to be indolent – 'this tract seems the residence of sloth' – and unable to feed themselves, with the result that many went to the east coast to assuage their famine, or emigrated.

Using a foot-plough, or *cas-chrom*, the people tilled small fields, 'many ... no longer than the floor of an ordinary room', to grow oats, bere and potatoes. To extend the cultivable ground, the crofters made the inaptly titled 'lazy beds' by gathering earth into one spot and enriching it with layers of dung, lime and seaweed. Potatoes appeared in the area around 1766 and soon became the staple item in the diet, supplementing the existing milk, whey, oatmeal and bere. 'Their best food is oat or barley cakes,' noted Bishop Pococke in 1760. 'A porridge made of oatmeal, kail and sometimes a piece of salt meat in it, is the top fare.' The poor land made the sea fisheries all the more crucial to well-being: 'Every man is a fisher and fishes for himself.' The herring catch must have seen many a family through the winter, for the crop harvests were often insufficient and had to be supplemented with meal imported from Caithness.

This harsh, impoverished way of life, more extreme in the north-west than elsewhere in Caithness and Sutherland, was the forerunner of crofting. Now regarded as part of the traditional way of life of the Highlands, crofting in its present form was more or less created by Act of Parliament in 1886, after the Napier Commission presented its final report. Other Acts followed the Crofters Holdings (Scotland) Act, and to supervise the considerable body of crofting law the Crofters Commission was eventually established in 1955 with its headquarters in Inverness. Legal disputes are settled by the Scottish Land Court. There are at present about one thousand registered crofts in Caithness and just under two thousand in Sutherland. In recent years crofters in the two counties have received substantial grants for improvement, and several thousand acres of land have been reclaimed. Much more awaits the ditching machines and the pipe-layers. Land that has lain fallow since the Clearances and parks that have been re-invaded by rushes and heather could once again be put to the plough.

The word 'croft' properly refers only to the land that a crofter farms: his or her house, steading, fences, drainage and other improvements remain the property of the crofter, which have to be compensated for should the croft be given up. Also, a crofter is entitled to determine who shall inherit the croft, and has the right to sublet. The landlord has the right to apply to take back the croft but his request has to be approved by the Land Court, who determines any compensation to be paid. In addition to the acres tilled or for pasture, a crofter has certain rights to share common grazings which are usually managed by locally elected committees. Much of the old communal life of the townships is preserved in the modern crofting districts.

It is difficult to define a croft exactly. Everyone knows one when they see one, but in everyday speech the term is used loosely to describe agricultural holdings of several types. To quote one of the Crofters Commission publications: 'Whenever there is doubt as to whether a holding is a croft it is ... necessary to investigate the history of the tenancy from its origin.' Broadly speaking, a croft is of modest size and having a modest annual rent; it is common for at least one member of the crofting family to have a job 'off the farm'.

Between Rhiconich and Laxford Bridge lies the Rough Quarter, in Gaelic Ceathramh Garbh, a strange country of hummocks and lochs, more water than land, bare and open and windswept. Two miles to the south of Rhiconich a minor road turns off over the braes to Skerricha, tucked under the hills at the head of Loch a'Chadh-Fi. Close to here, John Ridgway established his School of Adventure at the end of the 1960s. The school takes its name of Ardmore from the crofting township on the north-west side of the loch, and runs courses in climbing, sailing, canoeing and other outdoor pursuits.

At Laxford Bridge, the A838 turns eastward to quit this rough land for Lairg. It creeps past Loch Stack under the crags of Ben Stack, swings south by Achfary Forest and then follows the long Loch More to Kinloch. From here it runs through the valley of Loch Merkland to the upper corner of Loch Shin, and thence south-eastwards to rejoin the A836 a few miles from Lairg.

The hamlet of Laxford Bridge is at the apex of Loch Laxford, a sea loch with a long, convoluted shoreline flanked with rows of reefs and small islets. Except for the little villages of Foindle and Fanagmore and a house or two at Badnabay, the shore is deserted; a sense of wilderness hangs over the water and the rocks, accentuated at low tide when birds pipe and strut on the bared muddy flats. The scene has changed little since the day when a Norse longship nosed in from the Atlantic and the loch received its name ('lax' is from the Norse for salmon).

The A894 runs west along the south shore of the loch. Beside Claisfearn it loops around Loch a'Bhagh Ghainmhich, whence a branch runs to Foindle, Fanagmore and Tarbet, where there is a little beach. The roads here are characterized by short, very steep gradients, like an asphalt switchback. Before the road was made, one traveller noted: 'It would be impossible to advance a hundred yards without danger from precipices or bogs' after sunset, and 'No man, who cannot climb like a goat and jump like a grasshopper, should attempt to travel' through the country.

Off the coast at Tarbet stands the island of Handa, now a nature reserve run by the Royal Society for the Protection of Birds. The island can be reached from Tarbet or from Scourie, three miles to the south. Handa was described in 1790 as 'the resort of vast numbers of sea-fowl'; today this is still true. The people of the area used this resource 'catching and killing great numbers ... to the benefit of their families in the way of provision'. Feathers were bartered for wool. In common with other islands, Handa offered a graveyard secure against the depredations of wolves before these animals became extinct. Seven families lived on Handa until 1848, tilling the ground for potatoes and catching fish and seabirds in the lee of the four-hundred-foot cliffs. The island became a reserve in 1962, and it is served by a full-time warden in the summer months.

The large scattered village of Scourie is an important centre, lying in a fold in the hills at the head of Scourie Bay. The pier, with its attendant small fleet of boats, is tucked into the sheltered north corner of the bay, at the end of a curving sandy beach, close to Scourie House in its grove of trees, among which are a palm tree or two. There is an extensive caravan park at Scourie, and in summer it is a popular tourist stop.

Scourie was the birthplace in 1640 of Lieutenant-General Hugh Mackay. He is probably best remembered for losing the battle of Killiecrankie, but he was a prominent officer in the army of William and Mary. He fell at the siege of Namur in 1692.

Soldiering occupied a major place in the lives of Highlanders until comparatively recently. Donald, Chief of Mackay, was knighted by James VI in 1616 and raised to the peerage, as Lord Reay, in 1627. A year before, he had raised two thousand men to fight in Bohemia in the Thirty Years War. Three thousand actually left Cromarty in October 1626 for Europe, where they ended up fighting for the King of Denmark. Several officers, judging from their surnames, were the sons of Caithness families. A German woodcut dating from 1631 shows four of Mackay's men: bearded, armed with bows and muskets, wearing tartan plaids and bonnets. Lord Reay himself died in 1649 in Denmark or perhaps in Norway – the exact location is uncertain – but his body was taken home and buried at Tongue.

The men of the north had of course been following their chiefs into battle for centuries. These conflicts were rarely of more than local significance but many men served abroad as mercenaries of foreign powers. Some nine hundred Caithness men, under the command of George Sinclair of Stirkoke, were massacred at the Pass of Kringelen in Norway in 1612, while on their way to join the army of the King of Sweden.

The Highland regiments hold a famous place in the annals of the British army. Between 1740 and 1815 eighty-six were formed, representing upwards of sixty thousand men, a high percentage of the region's youth. After the '45 Rebellion, Westminster, in its search for recruits, began to look north. 'I ... drew into your service a hardy and intrepid race of men,' William Pitt told the House of Commons in 1766; '... they served with fidelity as they fought with valour and conquered for you in every part of the world.' The Highlanders came forward to the colours in droves. Perhaps for some it was a love of soldiering and a belief that it was a noble thing for a man to do that encouraged them. Many enlisted to escape poverty and remitted money home to their families. And the tradition of answering the chief's call to arms lived on. However, there is no doubt that many took up arms reluctantly, at the behest of their chiefs, without understanding what they were fighting for.

In Strathnaver, at Skail, there is a stylized cairn marking the spot where the gathering to form the 93rd Sutherland Highlanders took place in September 1800.

The method for selecting men in the days of the Earl
of Sutherland [wrote Alexander Mackay] was for him
to call parochial meetings when all the males were
formed into regular ranks. The chieftain, or some
respectable individual acting for him, with a large
snuff box in one hand and an attendant with a bottle
of whisky, went along the ranks and to every young
man whom he wished to enter the corps, he ordered
snuff – the signal was perfectly understood – the
young man stepped out, took his snuff and dram, and
the clerk recorded his name and attestation. They
were then collected and the King's Bounty paid to
them until such time as they should be called up for
embodiment.

In 1800 the oficers raising the 93rd sent ahead of them for
distribution quantities of tobacco and snuff. The Reverend
Donald Sage observed that they need not have bothered as
'Smoking was a luxury then utterly unknown and quite
unappreciated by the men of Kildonan.' At the recruitment
parade 'the young men showed no reluctance to enlist' but
negotiation with their parents became a prerequisite: 'Two
things they were promised, first, that their fathers should have
the leases of their farms, and next that the sons, if they enlisted,
should all be made sergeants.' Neither promise was kept.

The behaviour of Highland troops was often in complete
contrast to that normally expected of soldiers. The inhabitants of
Plymouth were grateful and astonished when the Sutherland
Highlanders were seen to be spending more on Bibles and books
than on gin. While they were in Plymouth, the men sent over
£500 home to their relatives, many of whom were to be or had
already been evicted in the Clearances. However, as news came
through to the regiments of burning houses in their native
straths, and as the cynical attitudes of officers belied promises
made on enlistment, the troops reacted, sometimes violently.
The 2nd Sutherland Fencibles refused to move from Glasgow to
England in March 1794, even after a guinea was offered to each
man, because they had enlisted on the understanding that they
were to serve in Scotland. On another occasion, the Caithness
Fencibles, recruited by Sir John Sinclair of Ulbster, ran riot in
the streets of Berwick and beat up their adjutant.

The Clearances broke the old ties between chief and tenant. By the time of the outbreak of the Crimean War in 1854, 'the young men' were showing a marked reluctance to enlist. There is the famous reply of an old man to the second Duke of Sutherland demanding to know why no one was responding to the ducal call to arms: 'These lands are now devoted to rear dumb animals which your parents considered of far more value than men.'

From the beginning, the soldiers displayed tremendous courage in action. The battle honours of the regiments are virtually a rehearsal of Britain's wars in two centuries, and there is some truth to the boast that the Empire was built on the blood and bones of Highlanders. Recruitment still goes on, though on a much reduced scale: the principal regiment drawing on Caithness and Sutherland today is the Queen's Own Highlanders, based in Fort George near Inverness and formed in 1961 by the amalgamation of the Seaforth and Queen's Own Cameron Highlanders.

To the south of Scourie the road dips by Badcall Bay. Sutherland's first fish-farm was set up here in 1975 by Joseph Johnstone & Sons of Montrose. Employing about thirty people, the farm produces between four and five hundred tons of fresh salmon in a year, most of which is sold in Britain but some goes to Europe and the United States.

From Badcall the road runs through softening country past the Duartmore Forest to Kylestrome and Kylesku. This was the site of the famous Kylesku ferry, which went out of operation in the autumn of 1984, when the handsome new bridge was opened. On my last visit, from the ferry, *The Maid of Glencoul*, I saw two dolphins and a seal. I doubt if crossing to Assynt over the bridge will have the same relaxed air, but the bridge affords splendid views of the two lochs, Glendhu and Glencoul, arms of the sea reaching nearly four miles into the heart of the mountains. The deep sheltered water here was the scene of an important herring fishery in the early 1800s; £30,000 worth of fish were taken in the autumn of 1829.

Assynt begins on the south side of the lochs. The A894 continues directly southward over a high ridge of moorland to Loch Assynt. From Loch na Gainmhich near the top of the ascent from Unapool paths strike out over the hills to Eas a

Chual Alumn, at 658 feet the highest waterfall in Britain. The best view of the falls, however, is to be got by sailing up Loch Glencoul from Kylesku and landing at the head of Loch Beag. Eas a Chual Alumn is difficult to see from the landward side; the cascade is split into a series of steps which are dangerous to approach from above.

About two miles south of Unapool, the B869 branches off to the west to follow the coast around to Lochinver. It is a route to test a driver's mettle and a cyclist's puff. The tarmac throws itself like a suffering snake around and over the hills. There are vicious bends and gradients up to 1 in 4, but the country is breathtakingly beautiful. Wooded glades, as at Gleann Ardbhair and along the Allt a'Ghamhna, alternate with bare open moors and lochans; and the whole landscape is dominated by the great kist of rock of Quinag with its serrated ridge. Quinag is pronounced 'coonyag' and may be derived from the Gaelic *cuinneag*, meaning a milk churn; although the shape of the mountain may have put some people in mind of this domestic apparatus, there is little that is homely about Quinag. The highest peak reaches 2,653 feet.

Several small villages cling to the fringe of this rough country: Nedd, Drumbeg, Clashnessie. Drumbeg is the largest: there is a school here, a hotel and shops. Clashnessie lies at the root of the Stoer peninsula and marks a change in the landscape. Gneiss gives way to sandstone, and the more yielding rock has been eroded not into hummocks but rolling hills. Crofting townships – Achnacarnin, Culkein, Clashmore, Balchladich – make Stoer a relatively well-populated area.

A long, single-track road, with sensible gradients and bends, runs out to the unmanned lighthouse on the Atlantic side of the peninsula, where the surf pounds in on the red rocks. More often than not, the visitor's only company here will be gulls and sheep. The view to the south takes in the Coigach peninsula and the hills of Wester Ross. A bracing, two-mile walk will take one right out to the Point of Stoer, past the rock stack called the Old Man, frowning at the Minch, all 220 feet of him.

From the Stoer peninsula the B869 passes through Stoer itself and Clachtoll, and back onto a gneiss landscape, back to short, steep braes and blind curves. At the crests of the hills, the southward-bound traveller will receive views of the Assynt area behind Lochinver and the sugarloaf peaks of Suilven and Canisp looming on the horizon. In the oceanic climate the peaks are frequently bewhiskered with cloud. On rainy days they disappear altogether and may remain hidden for some time until the cumulus thins and once more they drift, like galleons, into view.

Close to Achadhantuir, a minor road leaves the B869 and leads down to Achmelvich. There is a youth hostel here and a caravan site, where wind-blown sand from the beach supports green machair. Off the coast, over the sandy patches the sea shines with an opalescent milky green, turning to the colour of claret over the seaweed beds; further out, on a clear day, you can see the Hebrides, beyond the Minch where the deep blue sea is fretted with white. Achmelvich is such an attractive spot that it has almost been destroyed by tourists. The machair, much prized by the crofters as pasture, is a fragile skin, and once the turf is broken by wheels or too many feet the wind can get in below it and blast it away. The danger was recognized in the early 1970s, and since then access has been controlled. Continual reseeding and returfing are preserving the machair. Local people sometimes see tourism as a necessary evil, not out of selfishness but because they know that a large influx of visitors is in danger of wiping out that which they come to enjoy.

The B869 joins the A837 on the outskirts of Lochinver. In 1831 this place was described as the only one in the west 'deserving the name of a village'; 'in it are some good houses, shops and several tradesmen.' There was also a post office and a savings bank here then. These sentences would serve well as a contemporary description of the village, though now it is much larger. It stretches along the shore between the mouths of two rivers, the Inver and the Culag. The river mouths are thick with luxuriant seaweed, but between them the sea tugs at a shingle beach. At the south end of the long street is the main harbour. Here seine netters chug in to land their catches and replenish their stores: the Pier Foodstore has a sign telling fishermen wanting groceries to ring a certain telephone number when the shop is closed. The pier is busiest on a Thursday afternoon, when the boats are landing fish before the market prices drop on Friday afternoon. As at Kinlochbervie, the majority of the boats are from east-coast ports. The pier was originally built at the beginning of the nineteenth century in two parts of stone and wood, and was maintained jointly by the Duke of Sutherland and David MacBrayne, the west-coast shipping owner. It has been extended twice in recent years, in 1969 and again in 1974. There is a lifeboat station, a Mission-house and cafeteria, the offices of the Lochinver Fishselling Company, a towering ice plant, and marts. A shellfish processing plant is also being built here.

Tourism is the other mainstay of the Lochinver economy. In summer the bay is alive with windsurfers and canoeists: 'No my cup o tea,' said a fisherman one day to me as we watched a windsurfer take a header into the grey water. It rains a lot in Lochinver. The day-trippers plod like flocks of wet hens, but the wet does not deter the school parties who head here for adventure training. Of course, there are plenty of days when the sun shines and the sea and the land sparkle with colour.

In Baddidarroch, to the north of the village, you can find the premises of Highland Stoneware Ltd, with fourteen employees one of the larger craft factories in the two counties. Founded in 1974, the firm makes and sells a full range of hand-painted pottery much of it for export to Europe and America. The potters have experimented with using local rocks to produce distinctly coloured glazes. Highland Stoneware is also the birthplace every fortnight of the *Assynt News*, a community newspaper that manages a circulation of over four hundred in a catchment area with a total population of 850. One hundred copies are mailed to exiles, one of whom said that it was. as good as a letter from home. The *News* began life as four sides of A4 paper on a duplicator on a dining-room table but it has grown considerably since then.

At the other end of Lochinver, a lush plantation to the south of Culag pays tribute to the Atlantic rains and the mild oceanic air. In the middle of the trees, on a boulder the size of a cinema screen, are cut the words: 'These woods were planted and these paths made by George Granville Second Duke and Twentieth Earl of Sutherland A.D. 1847.' The path under this proclamation leads on to a pebble beach, a quiet place of lapping waves out of earshot of the harbour, called the White Rocks after the belichened gneiss.

The teeming shoals of herring in the western sea lochs began to be exploited on a large scale in the last half of the eighteenth century. John Knox, a retired Edinburgh bookseller, made a tour of the coast on behalf of the British Fisheries Society in 1786. 'We had a pleasant evening's sail to the mouth of Loch Inver,' he recorded. 'The men complained as usual of the rise in their rents. "Our fathers," said they, "were called out to fight our master's battles, and this is our reward." They spoke with seeming indifference of the cause in which their fathers, and probably some of themselves had been engaged, which they said, they did not understand.' Knox and his companions stayed the night with Donald Ross, who had, with a Manx entrepreneur called Joseph Bacon, built in 1775 a fishing station at the head of the loch with 'a large curing house'. The visitors noted that the inner loch had 'a fine clean entrance, with twenty fathom water, which lessens gradually towards the head, where there is above five fathom, and a fine sandy beach, near to which the herrings are taken'.

The fishing station was flourishing forty years later, when two Englishmen, Richard Ayton and William Daniell, paid a visit. The proprietor of the station had a walled garden with an orchard yielding 'a fair crop of apples, pears, cherries and small fruit of various kinds'. The fishing boats, the labourers and the coopers hammering at their barrels created such a 'bustle and activity' that Ayton found them to be 'an agreeable contrast to the dreary stillness' of the land around them. Near here, Ayton also heard a story about an old woman called Mhoir Bhein who lived at Ru Stoer in the 1760s: she was reputed to be a witch and held to steal milk from the udder, sink ships at sea and go about as a grey cat. Some local lads strangled her with a halter, for which crime they were later tried and acquitted: Janet Horn was not the last person to die in Sutherland on a charge of witchcraft.

From Lochinver a narrow, twisting road threads it way past the villages of Strathan, Badnaban and Inverkirkaig to the District boundary of Sutherland on the River Kirkaig. The latter is a lively stream, perhaps ten yards wide, rushing seaward through a narrow, wooded glen. On the south side are Wester Ross and the Inverpolly National Nature Reserve. Hard above the stream on the Sutherland side is the Achins Bookshop, run now by Alec and Agnes Dickson. Alec gave up a job as a civil engineer to start business here in 1983 and has not regretted the move.

Where the Kirkaig enters the sea, there is a sand and shingle beach backed by some small fields and gardens. It is also worth mentioning that beside the beach a bar called the Valhalla awaits the thirsty traveller. A path along the Kirkaig leads to a spectacular series of waterfalls three miles inland; and it is possible to walk in through the hills, under the flanks of Suilven, to Elphin.

The main road from Lochinver, the A837, runs inland from the north end of the town. This highway has been straightened and improved in recent years, and the loops of the old road, like ox-bows of asphalt, and its small bridges remain beside the new one as a reminder of the difficulties of travel in this terrain, where every hummock appears to be trying to emulate the soaring masses of Suilven and Canisp. The road skirts the northern shore of Loch Assynt. At Skiag Bridge it is joined by the A894 coming over the hills from Unapool.

Near the junction stands the ruin of Ardvreck Castle, built in the last decades of the sixteenth century by the Macleod lairds of Assynt. The Macleods gained Assynt in the fourteenth century and held land here until they were ousted by the Mackenzies of Kintail in the later seventeenth century. Perhaps the most notorious of the chiefs to occupy Ardvreck was Neil Macleod. He was in power in 1650 when the Marquis of Montrose, fleeing in peasant's clothing from the carnage of Carbisdale, came over the hills to the west. Macleod is reputed to have been the one who betrayed the Marquis to government troops, perhaps motivated by the thought of the reward. If this were so, Macleod was hard done by, for it is said that he received for his treachery forty bolls of bad oatmeal and nothing else.

There is not much left of Ardvreck today. The most intact part of the tower is the south-east corner; rubble fills much of what is left of the interior, but the vaulted ceilings of the cellars can be seen. The castle was destroyed by fire after the estate had been taken over by the Mackenzies – and thereby hangs another colourful legend. The occupiers of Ardvreck held a ball that continued long into a Sunday. To avoid an end to the frolicking, the dancers drew the blinds and cut the tongue from a cockerel so that they would not know when their night of revelry was coming to an end. A dispute arose among the guests, and the Devil was invited to arbitrate. The company began to chant the Devil's name, but when he appeared, he came with such force that he set the castle afire, and the building was consumed within minutes.

There is a chambered cairn on the spit of land behind the castle, and half a mile away on the shore of the loch are the double-pointed gables of Calda House. This was a residence of the Mackenzies, and it too was burnt, in the early eighteenth century by Macraes from Kintail. The Mackenzie estate was declared bankrupt in 1739; after the '45 Rebellion it was bought by the Sutherlands and remained in the possession of the Earl and then the Duke until 1913.

Inchnadamph stands at the head of Loch Assynt. On a knoll here, between the road and the school, there is a memorial to two scientists, Ben N. Peach and John Horne, who first investigated the complicated geological structure of the north-west between 1883 and 1897.

The north-west of Sutherland is the oldest part of Britain, and its exposed rocks of Lewisian gneiss, formed up to 3,000 million years ago, are a mecca for geologists. The geology is exceedingly complex, and the devotee can find detailed descriptions in specialist publications. The metamorphic, hard, crystalline rock on the west coast is overlain by bands of younger rock to the east. The peaks of Suilven and Canisp are composed mainly of Torridonian sandstone – at 750 million years, the oldest sedimentary rocks in Britain. Cambrian and Ordovician limestones and mudstones make up a band underlying a strip of fertile ground running from Durness to Elphin. The rock beds are intensely folded and metamorphosed, particularly in the vicinity of the Moine Thrust Zone, extending from Whiten Head to Elphin, where younger rocks have been thrust westward over older deposits. The structure is complicated further by intrusions of igneous rocks such as granite.

A geological map of the area hangs in the public bar of the Inchnadamph Hotel so that drinkers can discuss over a dram Cambrian limestone or perhaps the thrust folding of dolomite. There are also pictures here of speleological expeditions in the local limestone cave systems, and a plan of a nine-hole golf course that, at the turn of the century, was laid out beside Ardvreck.

Not far from the hotel is a little white-washed church, curious in that it has four dormer windows overlooking the graveyard. At the church gate there is a memorial to a RAF aircrew who lost their lives in a crash on Ben More Assynt in 1941. Inchnadamph also has a mountain rescue post.

The A837 continues south up the valley of the Loanan river under soaring limestone cliffs, past Loch Awe to the Ledbeg river and the village of Ledmore. There are chambered cairns in this area. A short way beyond Ledmore is the Altnacealgach Hotel, which we reached earlier, at the head of Strath Oykel. The optimism of the Age of Improvement led an English entrepreneur to open a marble quarry at Ledbeg early in the nineteenth century, but the venture failed after a short while. A short stretch of the A835 brings us from Ledmore to the district of Elphin at the head of Loch Veyatie, a green bowl of a place. About a mile and a half south of here the road leaves Sutherland and enters Wester Ross through a high, windy pass under frowning crags. To the west lie peat bogs and the peaks of Coigach and Cul More.

The north-west Highlands comprise an open, at times frightening, wilderness, a place where wind and pool and rock force their way into the spirit. It is far, however, from being a place without life. The ornithologist can expect to see over two hundred species of birds: common species like the kestrel, hovering over the moors; rarer waders, such as the greenshank. There is, in fact, a great diversity of habitat in Sutherland: large numbers of waders and waterfowl winter on the fertile firths and beaches while colonies of seabirds populate the cliff faces. The woods and forests, especially around the Kyle of Sutherland, support a variety of woodland birds, and moorland species enjoy a wide range throughout central Sutherland and Caithness. The coastal seas are still mercifully free of pollution: and seals and sea mammals are common, and the clarity of the water enables one even to watch fish.

The great auk, the wolf, the lynx and the beaver are among the species that are now extinct but which once were common here. On the other hand, the fulmar, which in 1912 was known only on Handa and Clo Mor, has increased in numbers until it is now among the commonest of seabirds. Some small birds, for example the great tit and the blue tit, have increased greatly in numbers this century.

A woodland of birch, rowan, hazel and juniper flourished over a wide area of the north in prehistoric times, but climatic change and human settlement disposed of most of it. The northernmost

stands of native pine forest are to be found around Amat in
Strath Carron and in Glen Einig, and fragments may exist on
islets in Loch Assynt where the surrounding water has protected
the plants from sheep. Among early references to forest in the
north is one in the *Laxdaela Saga*, which describes a longship
being built in a forest in Caithness in about AD 900. As late as
1506 the accounts of the Lord High Treasurer of Scotland record
£7 'to Schir Alexander Mackyson to his expens to pas in Caitnes
to get cut tymir for the Kingis schip'. This does not make clear
the part of Caithness concerned, but it was probably the
south-east and may have referred to the area of Dornoch or Loch
Fleet, all being considered part of the province of Kat, the
bishop's diocese.

The interior of the north-west, much of which has probably
never been heavily wooded, made up the great deer forest of
Reay, Diru Mor. Bishop Pococke wrote to his family in 1760 to
describe the hunt held by Lord Reay at Durness every August:
'They compute a thousand red deer in that country, and that
four or five hundred of them have been drove into this part by
about a hundred men who drive the mountains, and they have
shot sixty of them in a day.' As a hunting ground it fell into
decline some time after the introduction of sheep-farms, but the
Duke of Sutherland excluded sheep early in the nineteenth
century, setting aside sixty thousand acres of the parishes of
Durness and Eddrachilis as deer forest. The conversion of
sheep-walks to deer forests took place over extensive areas in the
Victorian era and was another source of complaint by and
eviction of crofters. A letter in the *Inverness Advertiser* in 1882
railed against 'the unreasonable extension of deer forests' and
the turning of fertile straths into 'the mere play ground of idle
sportocracy'. By 1892 over 200,000 acres of deer forest, about one
fifth of the county, were available in Sutherland.

From this, it will be clear that much of what outsiders
recognize as wilderness is, in fact, a man-made waste. Control of
the land still seems to elude those who live on it. There is also a
danger that conflicts of interest between developers and
conservationists, often with local people caught uncomfortably
in the middle, can lead to a situation hazardous to the
countryside. Much of the Highlands has been earmarked as
being of special scientific interest – too much, according to some,

who see the botanist and the birdwatcher almost as the successors of the sheep-farmers and the sportsmen.

In 1983 the Chairman of the Highlands and Islands Development Board voiced a concern that conservation could be seen as a 'dangerous form of paralysis'. Increasing acreages are also being bought by outsiders – pension funds, Dutch, Arabs – who are ignorant of and frequently care nothing about local customs and obligations. In 1983 Francis Keith of Durness described how local people did not know and could not find out who owned land in his area, although he knew 'they are all absentee and they are all European'. According to the 1981 edition of John McEwen's *Who Owns Scotland*, there are seventeen estates of five thousand acres or more in Caithness, amounting to over sixty-nine per cent of the county, and thirty-eight in Sutherland, accounting for eighty-four per cent of the land area. The largest estates belong to the Sinclair Family Trust and the Countess of Sutherland respectively – to that extent, at least, the past is still with us.

Much land could be reclaimed for some kind of agriculture. Other areas, with soil of very poor quality, are being developed as commercial forests. For example, Fountain Forestry Ltd own around fifty-four square miles in Caithness and Sutherland, about one third of which, at the time of writing, has been planted with sitka spruce, lodgepole pine and other species. The Forestry Commission also own large forests in the two counties.

On the first visit I made to the west of Sutherland, cycling, I experienced a strong sense of this land being a frontier. I still think of it to some extent in that way, as a place where living demands a certain toughness, a resourcefulness, a determination to hang in there and to resist the option of emigration. The price of food and petrol in the rural shops can be as much as twenty per cent higher than in lowland cities; unemployment is higher than the national average; medical services can be far away; and in some places children have to travel long distances to school. This is the price of living in a beautiful wilderness, and who has more right to a voice in how it is developed than those who experience it all year round?

The area around Inchnadamph forms a National Nature Reserve of some three thousand acres. And it is here, in the caves about the Allt nan Uamh, that I want to end this journey. For this place is also a beginning of sorts. In these caves the first hunters to penetrate this land after the Ice Age found shelter and a degree of warmth and left the marks of their feasting. Excavations in the 1920s uncovered bones of animals, including those of cave bears, reindeer and Arctic foxes, and human skeletal remains.

The caves lie at the base of a limestone cliff, high above the glen floor, on the south side of the burn. The only sound is the dripping of water. The walk up to the caves is a bit of a trauchle on a clammy day. The burn is frequently dry in summer, a feature of limestone country, but lower down near the road springs and pots feed a lively cascade and water the tanks of a salmon hatchery. Up at the mouth of the caves you can look up and down the length of the glen and out across at the scree slope and bracken opposite, and see no one. Inside, dry brown earth slopes into black tunnels. It would be fanciful to suggest that I was conscious of the spirts of the mesolithic hunters, but I knew they had been there, and that was enough.

Glossary

broch	archaeological term, a tower-like building dating from around the time of Christ and characteristic of that period in the history of northern Scotland.
darg	labour, toil.
dolo	a concrete structure used to build breakwaters. (This is not a Scots word; I think it is of Spanish origin. It is an engineering term.)
douce	genteel.
geo	(pronounced 'gyo' to rhyme with 'go') a narrow cove, or cleft in a cliff face. The word is derived from the Norse *gjå* and has been adopted in Scots and in Gaelic, where it is spelt *geodha*. It is sometimes spelt 'goe' in placenames.
glupe	the opening in the roof of a sea cave through which spray may be forced in a storm.
gurly	turbulent.
harl	pebbledash.
kist	chest (in the sense of a wooden box; it also means 'coffin').
kittle	whimsical, tricky. A kittle beast is one that is difficult to deal with.
machair	(Gaelic) the pasture land that forms on sandy soil in the proximity of a beach.
skelp	large area (this is not the usual meaning of the word, which is 'slap' or 'blow', but it is used in reference to areas of ground in Caithness speech.)
trauchle	a task involving some degree of toil.

NB: some of these words can have more than one meaning, according to context, but I have given the meanings as I have used them.

Index